TV: The Most Popular Art

For my parents,
Horace and Bernice Newcomb

TV:
The Most Popular Art

HORACE NEWCOMB

ANCHOR BOOKS

ANCHOR PRESS/DOUBLEDAY
GARDEN CITY, NEW YORK

The Anchor Books edition is the first publication of
TV: THE MOST POPULAR ART.
Anchor Books edition: 1974

Library of Congress Cataloging in Publication Data

Newcomb, Horace.
   TV: the most popular art.

   Bibliography
   1. Television programs—United States.
   2. Television broadcasting—Social aspects.
I. Title.
PN1992.5.N4   791.45'0973
ISBN 0-385-03602-7
Library of Congress Catalog Card Number 74-3559

ACKNOWLEDGMENTS

I would like to thank Gwin Kolb, Norman Maclean, and Richard Stern of the University of Chicago, for their assistance during my period of study there. I would like to thank John Cawelti, also of the University of Chicago, for his guidance and continued assistance in my study of popular culture. The number of references to his own work that appear in the body of this book is only a slim expression of appreciation which must be paid by anyone who chooses to examine the popular arts in America. To Richard Dyer MacCann, of the University of Iowa, I express special thanks for encouraging this study and for reading portions of it in manuscript. His comments and criticisms have made it a stronger work.

A special group of friends have aided at various times and places, in various ways, with the production of this book. To Scott and Ann Colley, Paula Weiland, Steve Weiland, Curt and Mary McCray, Jo and Ed Orser, and Jim and Ginger Arnquist, then, I express sincere thanks.

My students have contributed greatly to this book. In classes at Cornell College, Saginaw Valley College, and the University of Maryland, Baltimore County, in conversation and in their own work, they have offered ideas of their own and served as critics of mine. I am grateful for the exchange.

For the help of my wife, Sara, there are no adequate expressions of thanks. Quite simply, the book would not have been written without her. For Jud and Kate, who have brightened my life while they may have lengthened my workday, I say it was more than worth it. I only hope that this book will make television something better for them to enjoy.

HORACE NEWCOMB teaches American Studies at the University of Maryland, Baltimore County. He has contributed a number of articles to such periodicals as *Chicago Review* and *The Journal of Popular Culture* and was chairman of the popular culture section of the Midwest Modern Language Association meeting in 1972. Professor Newcomb is also a former television critic for the Baltimore *Sun*.

CONTENTS

CONTENTS

THE RESPONSES TO TELEVISION

This book is a study of television as a popular art. As with all the popular arts such an attempt poses problems precisely because the popular arts are so much more than art. Mass entertainment, advertising vehicles, expressions of cultural and social concerns, they exist in a perpetual tension between what will sell and what satisfies the multiple needs of producers, actors, writers, directors, and the audience. Perhaps with television, more than with other popular arts, there has been confusion as to purpose and definition. No one seems to know just what the medium is, and the estimates range from the prime impetus of massive cultural change to the narcotizing trap of American society. As a result, the responses to television are infinitely varied. Not only are the approaches widely different, but similar approaches often emphasize different factors and result in different conclusions.

In all of the analysis generated by the existence of television, however, little attention has been paid to television as a form of popular art, as mass entertainment. Television criticism in daily or weekly form comments on television drama, and there are numerous shorter studies of various artistic aspects of the medium. But the lack of a full study of television in these terms is the stimulus for this book.

Before beginning, however, we must examine the

other forms of television commentary, the varied responses to television, in order to learn what they have and have not told us.

The Visionaries

In the beginning no one knew what it would be. One reporter, covering the 1939 New York's World Fair, at which television was publicly introduced, had this to say:

The problem with television is that the people must sit and keep their eyes glued on a screen; the average American family hasn't time for it. Therefore, the showmen are convinced that for this reason, if for no other, television will never be a serious competitor of broadcasting. [New York Times, March 19, 1939]

We smile now, of course, but hindsight is cheap. It is not so easy to laugh at believers who erred in supposing that the new medium would direct life in a fresh, utopian direction. In 1946 Thomas H. Hutchinson wrote a book called *Here Is Television: Your Window to the World.* Essentially it is a book that explains how television operates, but in his introduction Hutchinson was willing to go far beyond simple technical description.

Television means the world in your home and in the homes of all the people of the world. It is the greatest means of communication ever developed by the mind of man. It should do more to develop friendly neighbors, and to bring understanding and peace on earth, than any other single material force in the world today.

Hutchinson did not thoroughly elaborate on how this would happen, but another technician, Lee De Forest, one of the developers of the medium, did. The concluding chapter to his book *Television: Today and Tomorrow* (New York, 1942) is entitled, "Television's Future and Its Influence upon Society." De Forest's concerns there touch a variety of topics. He speculated on information and education, on art and entertainment, on technological uses and social benefits. All, he concluded, can be enhanced by television.

He saw, for example, families gathered about the set in their own versions of "fireside chats." And from these strengthened ties might come the "betterment of our national life" (p. 348). Admitting that much of radio programming could be termed "banal, moronic—'bedtime stories'—to which are directly attributable neuroses among our children," he felt that television would be different because it would be visual as well as aural. "One may dare a blind song, venture a wisecrack, a banality—the artist well knows this could not be tolerated if he were beheld by his listeners. I foresee that self-censorship in television programs will be severe" (ibid.).

It seemed even more likely to De Forest that television would serve greater goals as a conveyor of fine dramatic art. Here De Forest did not rely on his own judgment, but quoted that of another visionary, albeit one with a vested interest, David Sarnoff.

A first-class radio program is like no theatrical or motion picture presentation that ever was. It is a new thing in the world. Similarly, it is quite likely that television drama will be a new development, using the best of the theater and motion pictures, and building a new art-form based on these.

It is probable that television drama of high caliber and produced by first-rate artists will

materially raise the level of dramatic taste of the
American nation, just as aural broadcasting has
raised the general level of musical appreciation.
[Pp. 350–51]

The point here is that for the visionary it was not
enough to bring drama to the homes of people who
might or might not wish to enjoy it. The new medium
had to be cast in the role of acculturizer, changing
the taste of the masses who would purchase sets produced by Sarnoff's corporation and later watch entertainment created by NBC. If this be self-justification,
we can return to De Forest for a purer sense of
idealism.

Citing the technical capabilities of television, for
example, he saw the new medium as an aviation aid,
as a direction guide and terrain altimeter, and as an
aid in weapons technology, optics, and electron mi-
croscopy (pp. 352–53). He saw it being used to bring
tours of art galleries into homes. Even in "crass commercial fields" he saw advantages. "As a medium for
showing to the housewife at night the models of dress
and hat to go on sale next morning, television will
prove the most effective sales agent in the history of
merchandising. And if shapely mannikins parade or
cavort before the iconoscope the male element of the
household will also sit up and take lively interest.
Tight pursestrings will be relaxed!" (p. 354).

Again, it is our own perspective that allows us to
see the ridiculous element in De Forest's glowing perceptions. But there is a sublime element as well, and
here our hindsight replaces laughter with a chilling
realization of what might have been. De Forest insisted, finally, in seeing television as part of a huge
pattern. His was a vision of American culture in
transition, moving upward on an evolutionary scale.

He pointed to the shortening workweek. He saw, incorrectly, an increasing emphasis on advanced age groups, predicting that by 1980, 35 per cent of Americans would be in the age group over forty-five years of age. That emphasis would lead, he felt, to a new emphasis on the meaning and experience of maturity. He saw a decentralization of industry and industrial populations. As people moved from "the congested cities to the metropolitan and surrounding rural districts," the skyscraper would become a thing of the past, and we "would note a gradual razing of these ridiculous structures, no more to be proudly exploited. Those impressive skylines must eventually subside" (pp. 355–56).

In the end television would be a vital part of a new world.

A population which once more centers its interest in the home will inherit the earth, and find it good. It will be a maturer population, with hours for leisure in small homes, away from today's crowded apartments. Into such a picture ideally adapted to the benefits and physical limitations of television, this new magic will enter and become a vital element of the daily life.

This new leisure, more wisely used, welcoming the gifts, entertaining, cultural, educational, which radio and television will bestow, shall eventually produce new outlooks on life, and new and more understanding attitudes toward living. [P. 356]

What a remarkable and enchanting picture! Obviously it is far more reflective of De Forest's own dreams and wishes than of any realistic social prediction. It is also reflective of a powerful and widespread cultural attitude and desire, for De Forest's dream is an accurate description of one of television's most frequently seen formulas. The happy suburban families appear on television. Their children may be unruly at times, but fathers and mothers with "new and more understanding attitudes toward living" ultimately manage to remedy any situation. Television has not changed our lives in the ways De Forest would have preferred, but the fantasy he projected remains with us.

Because we are fully aware of the gap between our own lives and the lives of those happy, fictional characters we see on television, it would seem safe to say that the visionaries were wrong and that they are no longer with us. To do so would be sorely to miss a major point. The newer visionary is not so concerned with what we see as with how we see it. He is concerned with television—or any other technical innovation—as a cultural object, as a device that, in itself, can change the ways in which we live. In the words of a contemporary visionary, it is not the content of television that counts, but the medium. "The medium is the message."

Marshall McLuhan is our foremost contemporary visionary. And it is good that we dealt with the older ones first, for they make it clear that McLuhan and his followers and friends are not so removed from the general sense of reality as might first seem to be the case. De Forest and Sarnoff were not so different from these latter-day media theorists. For McLuhan the key to television is that it restores mosaic perception. In is not uniform, repeatable, fragmented, or linear. It fosters depth perception in which the viewer is forced to pore into the object, first in order to see it, then in order to participate in it. He, too, sees television touching the small aspects of our daily lives; "the stag line, the party line, the receiving line, and the pencil line from the backs of nylons" are gone because of TV (*Understanding Media* [New York, 1964], p. 321).

McLuhan attributes to the power of television such cultural shifts as growing American concerns for the novelties of new foods and wines, for small cars, and for skin diving, activities that "involve" them more. He sees it touching the ways in which we choose to appear. "The TV extension of our nerves in hirsute pattern possesses the power to evoke a flood of related imagery in clothing, hairdo, walk and gesture" (ibid., p. 328).

If McLuhan had chosen to let his observations on the cultural results of television remain at this level, he would undoubtedly have been found interesting, but not particularly provocative or threatening. Like other visionaries, however, he sees television as a far more important force, one that changes the entire world, that shifts sensibilities and transforms human consciousness. He admits its importance in politics, for example. "Potentially, it can transform the Presidency into a monarchic dynasty. A merely elective Presidency scarcely affords the depth of dedication and commitment demanded by the TV form" (ibid., p. 336). Similarly, in education, "The right approach is to ask, 'What can TV do that the classroom cannot do for French, or for physics?' The answer is: 'TV can illustrate the interplay of process and the growth of forms of all kinds as nothing else can'" (ibid., p. 332).

But the classroom use of television is minimal compared to the ways in which it acts as an educative force simply by its presence in homes. McLuhan sees it changing the ways in which human beings think about themselves and their relation to the world they live in. The ultimate result of the new electronic media is a form of synesthesia, "or unified sense and imaginative life" which "had long seemed an unattainable dream to Western poets, painters, and artists in general" (ibid., p. 315).

The old print-based vision is crumbling under the influence of the new extensions of our consciousness. McLuhan, as a result, sees a return to tribalism, a concern with intimacy, the development of the Global Village. For Teilhard de Chardin, mystic priest and McLuhan's strongest co-visionary, the movement is a positive one, the ultimate development of biological evolution. The unity that will rise from such electronic connections will represent a true form of community, and more significantly, of communion.

Through the discovery yesterday of the railway, the motor car and the aeroplane, the physical influence of each man, formerly restricted to a few miles, now extends to hundreds of leagues or more. Better still: thanks to the prodigious biological event represented by the discovery of electro-magnetic waves, each individual finds himself henceforth (actively and passively) simultaneously present, over land and sea, in every corner of the earth. [*The Phenomenon of Man*, quoted in Marshall McLuhan, *The Gutenberg Galaxy* (Toronto, 1962), p. 32]

So it is that the old and the new visionaries are not so far apart. De Forest with his crumbling skyscrapers and burgeoning suburbia, his quiet homes with fireside chats, his renewed sense of intimate values, is Chardin's precursor. If McLuhan and his followers work on a global scale, one could say that it is because they have a clearer idea of the powers of the media and twenty years of experience with which to work. On the other hand, one might say that their sense of pride is simply larger. They are not content with the quiet nationalism of De Forest and Sarnoff, but seek to explain a new world order.

Common to both groups is a concern with the medium itself rather than with its content. True, Sarnoff and De Forest spoke more fully of content, but as with McLuhan the carrier is of prime importance. For this first generation of visionaries, questions of content related to an elitist concern with "taste." They sought to use television as a means of "improvement." For the second generation, the concern is with behavior. How will the audience "act" now that it has been exposed to television? What are the sensations caused by the medium? These are the crucial questions. In a way it is merely another kind of elitism. At the base of the vision of the new visionaries is a belief in the virtues they see occurring as a result of electronic change. Though McLuhan is quick to rule out moralizing, there are moral arguments throughout his work. For the visionaries, then, of both groups, television is part of a pattern of individual and cultural evolution, and the forces of that movement are ultimately beneficent ones.

The Social Scientists

For many observers, however, it took only a few years (perhaps, in some cases, only a few hours of viewing!) to decide that any cultural transformation brought about by television would be a negative one.

The social scientists are also concerned with the effects of television on an audience. They, too, are concerned, for the most part, with behavior and perception. Rather than emphasizing the cosmic consciousness, however, they concentrated on the minutely particular. They are more concerned with the number of acts of violence in a show, during an evening, or a week than with the ways in which those acts are surrounded with other factors. They are concerned with the time spent viewing and with the patterns surrounding the viewing. They are concerned with what the audience thinks it sees. All of these concerns are defined in ways that make them more easily quantifiable for study and comparison.

Some of them reduce the works of television entertainment art to absurd levels, ripping action, character, and motivation out of any semblance of dramatic context. Others, the best of them, carefully construct studies that are of immeasurable value to all other students of television.

Their concerns with the particular do not prevent them, finally, from arriving at some rather large conclusions, and in their own way, they approach the level of generalization often associated with the more free-wheeling media theorists. Dr. Eugene David Glynn, for example, produced in 1956 a massively general statement that has been cited in some fashion by almost every major study of television since that year. In "Television and the American Character —A Psychiatrist Looks at Television," Dr. Glynn reached some far-ranging conclusions. He begins somewhat "clinically."

Certain types of adult illnesses—particularly the depressions, the oral character neuroses, the schizophrenias—and the use they make of television can be most valuable here. Those traits that sick adults now satisfy by television can be presumed to be those traits which children, exposed to television from childhood (infancy, really!), and all through the character forming years, may be expected to develop. [William Y. Elliott, ed., *Television's Impact on American Culture* (East Lansing, Mich., 1956), p. 177]

After offering clinical examples of "adult illnesses" Glynn extracts a set of needs that television is supposed to satisfy. These, he says, are the ones we can expect to see develop into character traits by heavy television viewing. The examples, he says, could be multiplied.

They all demonstrate quite clearly the special set of needs television satisfies, needs centering around the wish for someone to care, to nurse, to give comfort and solace. . . . These infantile longings can be satisfied only symbolically, and how readily the television set fills in. Warmth, sound, constancy, availability, a steady giving without ever a demand in return, the encouragement to complete passive surrender and envelopment —all this and active fantasy besides. Watching these adults, one is deeply impressed by their acting out with the television set of their unconscious longings to be infants in mother's lap. [Ibid., p. 178]

Glynn, who like the visionaries cited the "form" of television as more important than content, admitted that there were other forces at play in the television viewing complex. The positive features of television, such as information, education, and the broadening of horizons, would be strong counters to the development of traits that he found detrimental to the national character, but these would require parental guidance and careful monitoring of the child viewer. Glynn sees television as both cause and effect, stimulus and response. His initial premise—that one discovers in disturbed adults the traits that will be fostered in healthy children—is highly suspect. And it should be noted that his is not the sort of analysis most often conducted by the social scientists. It does, however, indicate the sorts of concerns that the more reliable students seek to corroborate or disprove.

The best studies of television conducted by social scientists are far more careful in approach than is Glynn's. They are not given to such sweeping generalizations. They marshal evidence which includes the modifying characteristics tossed off so lightly in his analysis. Others limit their experiments to small, measurable topics, and when these studies are used in order to balance one another, we begin to see a clearer picture of television's effects on its audience.

Harry J. Skornia's *Television and Society* (New York, 1965) is one of the most comprehensive surveys of television in a social science context. Although there are no behavioral studies conducted by Skornia himself, there are surveys of and references to most of the major studies conducted before 1965. Skornia's own contribution is to place these studies within a complex web of other issues with which he is familiar as a student and historian of broadcasting.

Unfortunately, Skornia's book is a polemic. He fears the results of television and tells us so in honestly moralistic ways. He also marshals the evidence of other, statistically oriented social scientific studies to point to the detrimental effects of television viewing. He is concerned with both content and form, with the total package of watching television. He brings to bear almost any study that indicates that these effects harm individuals and create mob behavior. At times his arguments rest more on the juxtaposition of ideas than on logic. "But to those who have seen other masses created and manipulated," he says, "the way in which our media create and wield masses is strangely disquieting and ominous. Only thirty years ago masses assembled in the sports arenas in Nuremberg or Berlin, shouting *Sieg heil* with spine-chilling monotony" (p. 139).

A much more moderate and thorough survey is Leo Bogart's *The Age of Television,* written in 1956. Bogart, too, is concerned with surveying all the relationships involved in television. His work is heavily statistical, again using the studies of others to corroborate his own ideas. But here the ideas are not as blatantly moralistic and polemical as are Skornia's. He is careful, for example, to place the content of television within the context of mass taste, rather than to condemn outright that taste and suggest the supplementing of it with his own. He is careful in another way when he includes surveys of radio and newspaper influence, suggesting that television cannot be seen as the single influential factor in American life. The moderation involved in Bogart's study is best seen in his conclusion. Admitting many problems, defining some himself, Bogart finally decides that the early visionaries *and* the polemicists have been wrong. Though he wrote prior to Skornia, much of what he says could be applied to that work.

In its brief history television has become the American people's most important source of ideas, apart from interpersonal contact. It has changed the position of other mass media, and profoundly affected the way in which we spend our time with our families, and outside the home. It has influenced our outlook on the world and our political decisions, and it has an ever greater potential for doing this.

Yet television has wrought no violent revolution. It has not destroyed conversation or revived the intimacy of Victorian family life; it has not converted Americans from an active people into a passive one; its psychological effect on the young has not always been for the best, but at the same time it has not produced a generation of delinquents. Americans continue to work, play, make love, and raise children. Our world, in the age of television, is still the same world. But we experience it in new and different ways. [P. 331]

Both Skornia and Bogart study television in a total context, though they emphasize different factors. And both of them use the studies of other social scientists. Skornia to bolster an argument, Bogart to examine the studies side by side. The studies themselves indicate that Bogart's is the sounder of the two conclusions.

Of the thousands of studies conducted on various discreet aspects of television's behavioral and attitudinal effects, I will cite only two. The first is *Television in the Lives of Our Children*, edited by Wilbur Schramm, Jack Lyle, and Edwin Parker (Stanford, 1961). The study is early, and has often been examined and questioned. Serious arguments have been made against it. Findings, however, range freely on either side of Schramm and indicate that like Bogart, the conclusions rest firmly on middle ground. Again, the study cites a multitude of factors at work in the television experience. The conclusion is that at most, television is an influence rather than a cause. It can induce violence. It can also minimize violence. It can create passivity; it can also create action.

Similar findings emerge from Gary Steiner's *The People Look at Television* (New York, 1963). Steiner sets out to measure not the effects of television, but the ways in which people formulate attitudes and feelings *about* it, and about what they see on it. Again, this study points to a multiplicity of attitudes, feelings, beliefs. The either/or situation emerges. Television can do many things; what it does do depends on a host of surrounding factors.

Both the visionaries and the social scientists have seen television as a thing, an influence in people's lives. They have sought to measure, predict, restrain, or foster aspects of that influence. Both groups have, in many cases, chosen to ignore the fact that television is a particular kind of thing, a particular version of influence. Though it is capable of various sorts of communication, television most often carries entertainment in dramatic form. It is an artistic medium, but it has not been examined as an art.

This is not to say that there have not been excellent studies of individual program types, or that some critics and scholars and social scientists have not admitted to and examined the nature of the popular arts. But this has never been the major thrust of the study of television. As Elihu Katz and David Foulkes put it, "It is a most intriguing fact in the intellectual history of social research that the choice was made to study the mass media as agents of persuasion rather than agents of entertainment" ("The Use of the Mass Media as 'Escape': Clarification of a Concept," *Public Opinion Quarterly*, 1969, p. 378). Seeking a bridge between empirically and humanistically oriented research, Katz and Foulkes suggest the major differences between the two.

One reason for the gulf, it may be suggested, is that while the mass media researcher was asking, "What do the media do to people?" the theorist of

popular culture—while no less interested in the
impact of the media—was asking, among other
things, "What do people do with media?" [Ibid.]

One factor that Katz and Foulkes do not emphasize
is that the humanistically oriented theorist of mass
media and popular culture often suffered from the
same sort of elitist bias that warps many studies by
social scientists.

The Culture Critics

In *The People Look at Television* Steiner approaches
the problem of elitism by saying that "it is probably
inevitable that programs catering to the 'mass taste'
are, for the intellectual, synonymous with 'vast waste'"
(p. 242). This is true for the culture critics, a group
of commentators from many fields who feel that the
"mass" destroys necessary distinctions, primarily in the
arts. As a result of this attitude, serious study of the
popular arts has often been ignored. At the base of
the attitudes of the culture critics are the same sorts
of elitist restrictions found in some social scientists
and in most of the visionaries. The critics know what
is good for the masses, and little attention is given to
the complex relationships among audience and entertainment. Arguments against the "mass entertainment,"
whether on television or in other forms, become arguments against the audience. This has been pointed
out by other, more sympathetic commentators on
culture.

Every person of common sense knows that people
of superior mental constitutions are bound to find
much of television intellectually beneath them. If
such innately fortunate people cannot realize
this gently and with good manners, if in their

hearts they despise popular pleasures and interests,
then, of course, they will be angrily dissatisfied
with television. But it is not really television with
which they are dissatisfied. It is with people.
[Sir Robert Fraser, at the Manchester Lunch Club,
May 17, 1960. Quoted in Steiner, op. cit., p. 244]

An explicit example of this attitude may be found in
Dwight McDonald's "A Theory of Mass Culture."
"There are good theoretical reasons why Mass Culture
is not and can never be any good. I take it as axio-
matic that culture can only be produced by and for
human beings. But in so far as people are organized
(more strictly, disorganized) as masses, they lose their
human identity and quality" (Alan Casty, ed., *Mass
Media and Mass Man* [New York, 1968], p. 23). Given
this premise it is only a short step that enables Mc-
Donald to say that in such a society, "its morality sinks
to that of its most brutal and primitive members, its
taste to that of the least sensitive and most ignorant"
(ibid., p. 24).

A somewhat milder view, but nonetheless critical
for it, comes from Ernest van den Haag.

In popular culture, however, "art" is all that Freud
said art is and no more. Like the dreamwork,
popular culture distorts human experience to draw
"substitute gratifications" or reassurances from it.
Like the dreamwork, it presents "an illusion in
contrast to reality." For this reason, popular "art"
falls short of satisfaction. And all of popular
culture leaves one vaguely discontented because,
like popular art, it is only a "substitute gratification";
like a dream, it distracts from life and from real
gratifications. ["Of Happiness and of Despair We
Have No Measure," ibid., p. 8]

Van den Haag admits his own elitism with a good heart in his conclusion, where he is willing to say that there is no way to tell whether or not masses of persons felt better or worse without the popular arts which he sees as so detrimental.

In answer to such attitudes some culture critics are willing to argue that the popular arts do indeed make most people happier and that they are to be praised for it. Some cite the ability of the mass entertainment forms as conveyors of high art and as creators of good fun on their own terms. Others see quality in the popular arts themselves, arguing that "escape" is necessary at times, that laughter and adventure are best found in the popular arts, and that they, too, are beneficial. Here is Russel Nye in the introduction to his history of the popular arts, *The Unembarrassed Muse* (New York, 1970).

The fact that the mass audience exists, and that the popular artist must create for it, are simply the primary facts of life for the popular arts. Popular art can depend on no subsidy, state, or patron; it has to pay its way by giving the public what it wants, which may not always agree with what the artist may feel to be the most aesthetically apt. Satisfying a large audience involves no less skill than pleasing a smaller or more sophisticated one; popular artists can and do develop tremendous expertise and real talent. A best-selling paperback is not *ipso facto* bad; a song is not necessarily worthless because people hum it; a painting is neither bad because many look at it with pleasure nor good because few do. [Pp. 6–7]

Such a view is refreshing, and Nye's history supports it. The difficulty that remains when one goes beyond history is with *how* to study the popular arts.

Some studies continue to rely on the techniques of the social sciences, utilizing content analysis to demonstrate what attitudes are represented and in what proportions. Although such studies are immensely valuable, they often omit recognition of the artistic construct within which the attitudes and values appear. At other times they omit study of the artistic tradition within which the work is constructed. The task for the student of the popular arts is to find a technique through which many different qualities of the work—aesthetic, social, psychological—may be explored.

Television as Popular Art

Because the popular arts are so powerfully social in nature, it is often difficult to understand how humanistic analysis, the processes by which art is most often studied, can be of any help. Many of the arguments we have surveyed so far have simply assumed that such analysis is less than helpful because the works to be studied are designed for commercial purposes, because they have been created by groups rather than by individuals, or because they do not seem to have distinctive aesthetic qualities. In spite of these attitudes, however, the popular arts have with increasing frequency become objects of serious study by humanists.

Even with this surge of interest in the popular arts on the part of humanists, however, television remains the most neglected, the most unexamined. To some extent this is doubtless due to the sort of social stigma attached very early to television by the cultural elite. Some people still refuse to have television sets in their homes. Others, though critical of general programming, are willing to use the medium to view the sports spectacles. Some are more generous and are quick to praise some aspects of TV: the news, the ability to gather material quickly and to provide hours or even days of special programming related to special events. Still others make a sort of hobby of their devotion to certain programs; they find a detailed knowledge of "Star Trek" a distinctive advantage at polite parties.

A clue to the response to television is offered by Abraham Kaplan in his essay "The Aesthetics of the Popular Arts." Kaplan defends the popular arts thoroughly, suggesting that they are valuable even when without "higher" purpose.

But if not, what then? Aesthetic judgment is one thing and personal taste is another. The values of art, like all else aesthetic, can only be analyzed contextually. There is a time and a place even for popular art. Champagne and Napoleon brandy are admittedly the best of beverages; but on a Sunday afternoon in the ballpark we want a coke, or maybe a glass of beer. "Even if we have all the virtues," Zarathustra reminds us, "there is still one thing needful: to send the virtues themselves to sleep at the right time." If popular art gives us pleasant dreams, we can only be grateful —when we have wakened. [Irving Deer and Harriet Deer, *The Popular Arts, A Critical Reader* (New York, 1967), p. 342]

That, of course, brings us to the central issue with television. There has always been some question as to whether or not we will waken from our sleep, from the pleasant dreams that may be without lasting virtue. It is this fear that has given rise to serious attacks on television, to countless studies of the physiological and psychological effects of the medium. It leads to a continuing fear that a nation possessed of a dream-like "television mentality" will soon develop. If people begin to judge their "real" world of experience by what they gather from the action of television fiction, we will all be in serious trouble. So goes the argument.

This point of view indicates an attitude toward television that is distinct from that toward other popular forms. The popular arts may be condemned as unfulfilling and addictive, but they will not be cited as subversive so long as it is indicated that the addiction is to mystery or romantic novels. After all, reading is an activity, whereas watching TV is, for most people, a highly passive mode of behavior. Similarly, no great alarm will be raised so long as the popular arts are most strongly represented by the movies, for the movies end and we all have to go home. Like reading, it is a form of activity limited in time, demanding some sense of action, and which interrupts other activities.

These fears are not without foundation. Because of its association with massive commercial interests, because it serves as the medium for deceptive advertising, television is obviously different from these other forms, which have discovered a new respectability since its development. Any student or critic should share the fear. Any viewer should be aware of the possible dangers of misleading advertising although we know that many of them are not. But none of this should allow us to overlook the aesthetic capabilities inherent in the medium itself.

In order to examine television from the point of view of aesthetic concerns, it is necessary to develop some method, some way of cutting into its complex structure. One such method is that of the study of television's formulas. Here the concept of formula is articulated by John Cawelti in his study of the Western.

A formula is a conventional system for structuring cultural products. It can be distinguished from invented structures which are new ways of organizing works of art. Like the distinction between convention and invention, the distinction between formula and structure can be envisaged as a continuum between two poles; one pole is that of a completely conventional structure of conventions—an episode of the Lone Ranger or one of the Tarzan books comes close to this pole; the other end of the continuum is a completely original structure which orders inventions—*Finnegans Wake* is perhaps the ultimate example. [*The Six-Gun Mystique* (Bowling Green, Ohio, 1970), p. 29]

Clearly, television is essentially a formulaic medium in terms of its entertainment. Even more than the mystery or Western writer who brings us no more than a few works about a single character, television repeats its formulas complete with the same characters, the same stars, sometimes for years on end. Even then, it is possible to see a character in a highly formulaic series such as "Perry Mason" for years afterward in reruns. Successful television formulas are widely copied by those producers who hope to cash in on the commercial success that accompanies them. The formulas that survive have wide appeal in a massive audience. Their special appeal is so wide, say the harsher culture critics, that there can be no artistic excellence. But in examining the popular arts, even from the aesthetic point of view, we should keep in mind that the discovery of such excellence is not our primary task. Cawelti puts it this way:

I would like to emphasize that the distinction between invented structures and formulas as I am using it here is a descriptive rather than a qualitative one. Though it is more likely, for a number of reasons, that a work possessing more invention than formula will be a greater work, we should avoid this easy judgement in our study of popular culture. In distinguishing invented structures from formulas *we are trying to deal with the relationship between the work and its culture,* and not with its artistic quality. [Ibid. Italics mine.]

The task, then, is to discover why certain formulas, the mystery, the Western, the doctor and lawyer shows, are popular in American television. But with television, there is another level of complexity, for we quickly realize that the television Western is more akin to the television mystery than it is to the literary Western. It is even possible to say that the television mystery or Western is more comparable to the television situation comedy than to the literary forms of either of those two standard formulas. Television creates its own version of the traditional popular arts.

The subsequent chapters explore the ways in which television changes and modifies traditional formulas, how it begins to create a sense of the "television formula" with its own cultural significance. Each chapter deals with a separate formula or with a group of related formulas. While we explore the sense of cultural significance, it is also possible to define a set of artistic techniques, aesthetic devices that contribute to some unique capabilities on the part of television. The things that television does best are directly related to the most formulaic and popular works. They are developed in various ways by the various formulas we examine and build to a set of possibilities that allow television, like other media, to go beyond the popular and into works of great artistic complexity and cultural significance.

For too long we have assumed that television is one thing. It is not. It is as rich and varied as our other forms of entertainment. Hopefully this study from an aesthetic and cultural point of view will help to fill one significant gap in what Charles A. Siepman refers to as "The Missing Literature of Television." He closes that essay with a call for a new kind of television criticism.

Let us by all means continue to find out all we can about what television "is." But there remains a larger task; to determine what it *should* be and take steps to bring it nearer to the heart's desire. We badly need, as counterweight to such "objective" studies, the stimulus and light of imaginative writing that sets television and its myriad facets in a broader context than that of a private enterprise and relates it to the time we live in and our true requirements of it. [Robert Lewis Shayon, ed., *The Eighth Art* (New York, 1962), pp. 224–25]

Expression of the heart's desire has often been the province of the arts. To bring television closer to it does not mean to impose one's will for the masses on the art form that entertains them. Our task is to find out where the aesthetic qualities of television come from in the culture that produces them, and to find out what those qualities might become in the future.

2

SITUATION AND DOMESTIC COMEDIES: PROBLEMS, FAMILIES, AND FATHERS

Lucy's daughter, Kim, arrives home to find her mother preparing for a date. She is thrilled that her mother is going out, and her pleasure is heightened by her mother's enthusiasm. Lucy has met a suave, handsome, polite man—everything a middle-aged television widow could wish for. In the next scene Kim meets the date at the door. Played by Robert Cummings, he is indeed everything her mother has indicated. The two of them make polite conversation until Lucy comes downstairs, reversing the classic pattern of parent waiting for daughter's dramatic appearance. Lucy is glowing in a new dress, her hair strikingly done. As the couple leaves, the daughter calls them back and explains to Bob that her mother is to be dealt with carefully and returned home at a reasonable hour, furthering the reversal of roles. Big laugh on the sound track. Kim waits up for her mother, who promises to tell all in the morning.

The following morning—scene shifted to the kitchen —Kim is having breakfast alone before Lucy's entrance. The milkman, a neighborhood gossip, arrives with the daily delivery. The daughter asks if he delivers Bob's milk. "Of course," replies the milkman, and he begins to supply frightening details concerning the young women who are in and out of the apartment at all hours. Kim is increasingly alarmed; the milkman is increasingly comic. He envies the bachelor's freedom, his lack of responsibility, and his consequent harem. With each detail he sighs with desire as Kim cringes in fright. As Lucy comes in for breakfast, Kim hurries out of the house. She rushes to her mother's office and there solicits the aid of Uncle Harry in a plot to protect her mother from the menacing Bob. They plan a dinner party that will demonstrate Lucy's "true" nature and consequently frighten away the deceiving bachelor.

The wolf is met at the door by Uncle Harry, who casually reveals Lucy's wedding gown, hung prominently in the coat closet. It is kept there, he explains, in perpetual readiness. While Lucy is out of the room, Bob is told that she is actually older than he had been led to believe and is quite hard of hearing. He will have to speak loudly to her. Kim, meanwhile, has prepared a plate of special canapés for Bob, spiked with great quantities of hot sauce and pepper.

The following scene is the classic: yelling, mugging, strangling, confusion, and the gulping of huge glasses of water, all to the accompaniment of riotous laughter supplied by the sound track. Following a commercial break, we return to the scene. There, in summary form, we learn that the problem has been remedied. All characters are present and apologetic, for Lucy has explained that Bob is an agent for a modeling firm and does indeed use his apartment for interviews. She had known this all along. Kim and Uncle Harry are somewhat chagrined, but all in all it was a funny show and no one was ever really worried. The fadeout comes to a cast enjoying one another's company and laughing at its own misunderstandings, laughing at itself.

This is television's own form of comedy. Its roots go deep, of course, to farce, slapstick, to the confused comedies of the eighteenth-century stage, to the raucous silent films, even to Punch and Judy. But it is a standard format for television. No season is without a supply of new versions, but no season removes all of its old faithful, star-supported series, either. So stable—and so staple—is situation comedy that it has given rise to the parallel form, the domestic comedy. The only other comic forms on television are the monologue, a form not essentially visual, and the skit, usually a parody in situation comedy form.

The fact that Lucille Ball has starred in some type of situation comedy for over twenty years, however, does not mean simply that the form is a profitable time filler. More than any other television personality, she has found herself in situations like that described above. How many times has the audience watched in delight as she leaves the boss's theater tickets in a suit destined for the cleaners, calls the police to search for the kidnapped chimpanzee which turns up asleep in the neighbor's house? How many times have we marveled at the responses, the wide-eyed mugging, the bawling tears, the gleam of conspiracy? And there is something here that goes deeper than a superficial level of appeal.

This form allows Lucy to excel and in it we find many of the elements essential to any understanding of television as popular art. It is a paradigm for what occurs in more complex program types, and its perennial popularity is probably due to the relatively simple outline it follows. There is something here that allows us to do more than enjoy and laugh. Something makes us "love" Lucy.

In the delineation of the elements of the formula present here we can discern a meaning that goes beyond the element of "story." As we have seen in

Chapter 1, the formula becomes the particular way of ordering and defining the world. Much of that ordering in situation comedy and in other television forms will have a strong sense of the "unreal." I suggest, however, that in situation comedy and in all of television there is the creation of a "special" sense of reality. The total effect of specific formulas is this reality. Each has its own meaning, its own structure, its own system of values. Indeed, as we will see later, to break with this reality is to create a new formula, and in some cases a new form of television art. We begin with situation comedy precisely because its rigid structure is so apparent and because we find elements there that will carry through to other television formulas. A shift in emphasis, of focus, a different tone, a different sort of content, and we may find many of these same elements in mysteries, Westerns, doctor and lawyer shows, and many others.

Like all television forms, situation comedy creates its own special physical world. In part the worlds are defined by what is economical and what is feasible depending on varying advertisers and budgets. The southern California locale, for instance, predominates because that is the home of the film industry. But because content must be molded to this world, the physical circumstances take on a primary importance in defining the special nature of the formulas. As we will see, any change in setting—a movement, a change in decor, in design—reflects a change in attitude and in the meaning of the formula. These physical limitations, though they appear to limit the possibilities, delineate a great deal of the formulaic meaning that we are searching for.

The situation comedy depends on the one-room set.

In the Lucy show recounted above, there are three of these sets: the living room, the kitchen, and the office in which Lucy and Uncle Harry work. For the eye of the viewer there is nothing of substance "between" these sets—that is, there is no concrete, physical world of things. Movement is always accomplished by means of a fade-out–fade-in sequence, and to move from house to office the viewer is never allowed to see the street, to "enter" a car or a subway. We see no houses, no yards, no trees. The formula is, in this sense, internal. We become accustomed to the shift in scenes that occurs during the commercial break.

Stylistically, the rooms that we see in situation comedy are stale with repetition. Always middle to upper-middle class in tone, they are carefully crowded with stuffed couches and comfortable chairs, coffee tables on which there are small "objects," and walls on which hang conventional paintings. Somewhere in the room is a passageway to another part of the house, a stairway or a door to bedroom or kitchen. Because the most important rooms are the living rooms and the kitchens, the sets frequently depend on the "modern" suburban arrangement of these rooms, and our eye is allowed to flow through a dining "area" connecting the two important rooms in one space. Bedrooms and baths are hidden in the recesses, though in the more "sophisticated" series such as the Dick Van Dyke show, we may be admitted to them. In "The New Dick Van Dyke Show" we may even see the star and his wife occupying a double bed, in contrast to the "old" show in which the couple discreetly slept in twins.

Such homes reflect prosperity but not elegance. The standard of living is based on comfort; the rule of existence is neatness. During the meal scenes there is always plenty to eat, and a teen-ager frequently opens a refrigerator to pour another glass of milk. There is shabbiness or disarray only when called for by the script, and in such circumstances care is taken to indicate that it is an arranged form of clutter; the audience is immediately cued by the laugh track and the opening shots that this episode depends on a rearranged set of physical expectations.

The severity of this middle-class rule is indicated for us by the upturned world of "The Beverly Hillbillies." There, in the midst of the millionaire's luxury, they reflect the values of rural America—or perhaps it is more accurate to say that they reflect the values of rural America as conceived by middle-class Americans. At any rate the mixture is decidedly more middle class as they insist on wearing their worn, but very neat and clean, overalls. Their food is exotic, true, but the recipes are from the mountains and stewed possum is a staple dish. Much of the show's success depends on the continuing praise of middle-class virtues and the rejection of luxury as a way of life.

When one thinks of the living rooms in which the shows are viewed, a mighty contrast comes to mind. Where, on the television programs, are the scattered magazines and newspapers; where are the stacks of toys left by rumbling children? Does anyone ever run out of milk? Such scenes and events do not appear for good reason. We are not concerned with characters and their homes as representations of what "we" are like, of what our homes are like. We are concerned with what happens to a set of characters, and only incidentally will that character's physical surroundings and his attitudes toward them reflect our own. Indeed, the television version of the American living-dining-kitchen complex reflects a sort of idealized version which many of the viewers would choose over their own if given the opportunity, a factor that takes on greater importance as we now discover what it is that happens in these rooms.

Formula

What, in "real" life, is a situation? More aptly, what in "real" life is not? It is a strange word with which to define a formula, to define a type of comedy. Clearly, it is not meant to be universally applicable or we could find ourselves with situation tragedies or situation mysteries. In situation comedy the situation is simply the broad outline of events, the special funny "thing" that is happening this week to a special set of characters. The characters will appear at the same time the following week in another funny situation which will be entirely nondependent on what happens tonight. In the Lucy show episode the situation might be stated as follows: a reversal of the parent (mother) protects child (daughter) situation. In such terms this is a totally undeveloped situation, but clearly it has humorous possibilities.

In one sense the elaborate development of situation as it occurs in the Lucy show is rather roundabout; some minutes and three scenes are required to establish the situation fully. These scenes are required to define this episode's comic difficulty. In another manner, however, producers take a more direct route with the "built-in" situation. What happens when a man discovers that his beautiful young wife is a witch with incredible supernatural powers? Anything happens, and with great regularity. As the idea begins to wear a bit thin, there is always the possibility of introducing the mother-in-law, delightfully increasing the humor of the "my mother-in-law is a witch" idea. Similarly, it is possible for the young couple to have a child who is also a witch and who uses her "powers" in a typically childish fashion. If such a situation seems too extreme, one can always populate Beverly Hills with a family of mountain folk or marry a liberated Jew to a liberated Irish Catholic. Shipwreck a couple of millionaires, an actress, a professor, and a young girl with their pleasure boat crew, an inane captain and his zany crewman, and leave them on an island for a few years.

In such form, however, these descriptions are only bald outlines. In order for the situation to develop into something resembling a story, two other elements common to the formula must be added: complication and confusion. The complicating element in the Lucy episode is Kim's discovery of the suitor's "true" nature. The show cannot remain the same from this point on. Given the situation, the daughter must take it on herself to protect her mother, and to do this she must enlist the aid of the uncle. His concern, adult wisdom, maleness, and age are crucial. Basically, the complication of any situation is any element that begins the events of the particular show. It comes early, as soon as possible after the situation has been established. In an episode of "Bewitched," for example, where the situation is built in, Samantha and her daughter, Tabitha, shop for a doll. When the mother goes to pay for the item, the salesman chats with the small witch, remarking that he would like to be a child again. The laugh track begins to chuckle in anticipation and is rewarded when the little girl wiggles her nose manually and the salesman gapes at himself in the body of a nine-year-old boy. In the action that follows we are taken through all the contortions of convincing Tabitha that the man really wishes to be a grown-up again so that she can remove the spell.

Complications in situation comedies may take many forms, but most generally they are involved with some sort of human error or mistake. The source of the complication on the Lucy show has to do with the daughter's well-intended attempts at protection, but it rises basically out of the misinformation of the milkman. He is the low-comedy character, sighing and dreaming of a fuller life as he offers detail after detail which seem to indict Lucy's date. With each tidbit the daughter gasps and the milkman leers. It is an eloquent scene and the audience can thoroughly enjoy both performances, for the audience knows that this scene is the one that will precipitate the action that follows. Similarly, we may be treated to errors of a more physical nature. When Lucy leaves a winning lottery ticket in her boss's trousers, it is to the great delight of the audience that she must follow them through the entire cleaning process, emerging at last stiffened with starch.

It is such action that I refer to as confusion, the heart of what is comic about situation comedy. Situation comedy, like most television formulas, does not conform to the artistic standards of "high" art in the development of action, character, event, and conclusion. Events, the things that "happen" in sitcom, are composed solely of confusion, and the more thorough the confusion, the more the audience is let in on a joke that will backfire on the characters, the more comic the episode. Individual shows are frequently structured on various layers of confusion that can be generated out of a single complication. Like parentheses within parentheses, the characters slip into deeper and deeper confusion. Expression and reaction follow complication, gesture follows reaction, slapstick follows gesture. The broader the element, the louder the laughter.

After Bob has gulped several glasses of water in his attempt to drench the fiery canapés, he runs for the door and escapes. Lucy, who still does not understand what has been created by her guardians, eats one of the spiked appetizers. Before her daughter and Uncle Harry can stop her—their attempts are elaborately comic gestures—she swallows it whole and begins to steam, reaches for a pitcher of water and drinks it down as the fade-out begins. This is what we have waited to see, this moment of ultimate confusion in which the star proves her ability to outmug the other members of her family. There is no development, the "plot" is not getting anywhere. There are simply characters involved with one another in confusing sequences. The only movement is toward the alleviation of the complication and the reduction of confusion.

At the center of the situation, complication, and confusion stand the characters of the situation comedy. They are cause and effect, creator and butt of joke, the audience's key to what the formula means. As we have seen, that formula allows for little real development, no exploration of idea or of conflict; the stars merely do what they have always done and will continue to do so well. The characteristics of these favorites, the things that identify them, cut across program types and create not individual actors, but situation comedy stars, a television unit. We expect these characters to behave in certain ways, and if we have our favorites—Lucy, Gilligan, Granny—they will more than likely do the same things, react in the same ways, within their stylistically individual manners.

Physically the stars are easy to identify. With the

rural exceptions they are young American suburban-
ites. Lucy's TV age is around forty or forty-five. In
her earlier shows she could not have been cast as over
thirty. Only the older Clampetts, of "The Beverly
Hillbillies," exceed this top limit, and their actions be-
lie their age as the "eternally youthful" Granny out-
does her grandchildren in physical prowess and
mental exasperation. As becomes such youth, the characters are beautiful and healthy. They match the
neatness of their living rooms, and if the opening shots
of a show depict a character as ill or frazzled, we
know that it is called for in the script, that the situation depends on it.

All the characters are prosperous enough to afford
their suburban "ranch-style" homes. The husbands are
employed as advertising account executives, young
lawyers, or doctors. Dick Van Dyke in his earlier show
portrayed a comedy writer for a television variety
show, and Jeannie's husband is a career officer in the
Air Force. As with sickness, extreme fatigue is almost
always a function of the script. These people simply
do not work themselves out of the sitcom "look."

Emotionally, the characters correspond to this same
standard. They are never troubled in profound ways.
Sorrow cannot touch their lives. Stress, as the result
of confusion, is always funny.

Surrounding these central characters are two sets of
supporting characters. They offer a more natural
spread of types. In some cases they are older or
younger than the central characters—Uncle Harry and
Kim in "The Lucy Show," for example. In other cases
they are not as carefully "beautiful"; Miss Jane, the
secretary, in "The Beverly Hillbillies" is typical of
this class. Children of various ages, occasional
cousins, aunts, and uncles appear as needed.

One group of supporting characters is almost incidental. These people most nearly represent the audience. They appear in shops, banks, or offices. They are run over by fleeing characters, amazed and bewildered by unnatural events and unusual circumstances. Though they "populate" the comedy world, they almost never realize what the "situation" is, and they are often victims of the central characters' foibles.

More important is the set of regular characters who serve as foils for the antics of the stars. Ricky Ricardo and Fred and Ethel Mertz, of the "I Love Lucy" series, fall into this category. So do Ann Marie's father and her boyfriend Don in "That Girl." Banker Drysdale and Miss Jane, of "The Beverly Hillbillies," are classic patterns for the type.

Given such solid established worlds, it would seem strange that the characters should find themselves in difficulty. But difficulty is a mild word for the confusion that reigns in this formula. Again and again we run into horrible complications, plots involving policemen and postmen, mistaken identities and misplaced objects. Our middle-class characters come into possession of clues threatening gangsters, or formulas for secret weapons. Though the gangsters turn out to be funnier than guys and dolls and secret weapons fizzle in actual tests, it seems for the moment that we are beset on all sides by maddening complexities and problems. Ultimately, this is because of the most prominent aspect of the central character's makeup, a lack of any sense of probability. They are, in some way, out of touch with our day-to-day sense of how things happen, with the set of laws that allows us to predict the outcome of our actions. Again, Lucy is the prime example. She has no such sense of probability—not be-

cause she is stupid, for her schemes demonstrate exactly the opposite, but because she is innocent. Gilligan and Ann Marie are similar examples. They are
without malice, and if their actions precipitate a chain
of events that weighs heavily on other characters, it
is not because they are cruel, for just as often they
suffer the consequences themselves. Indeed, as often
as not they do not "do" anything, but act "naturally"
and are consequently done to. What they lack, or
what they refuse to recognize, is a knowledge of the
order of the world. If one did not suspect that the
word had been invented precisely for the advertising of a new situation comedy, they would have to
be called "wacky."

The supporting characters live somewhere between
the improbable world of the central characters and
the world as most of the audience experiences it.
Uncle Harry knows that his suit is very wet after Lucy
tips the water cooler over him, but it is unlikely that
he will break her jaw in response. It is probable that
the humor of the formula would be apparent simply
in the audience's comparison of the events of the show
with the events of its own world. There is no doubt,
however, that the placement of a set of characters
in the show, who will react similarly to the audience,
is an advantage.

Such characters are all the more important in the
show that depends on the built-in situation. If the
fractured sense of probability is a workable component, if the audience accepts a Lucy innocent of the
consequences of her own actions, then there is no
need for central characters to conform to the laws of
probability and reality in any way. It is only a short
step, then, to a world in which the suburbs are inhabited by witches and genies, and a shorter step still

to rich hillbillies in a Beverly Hills mansion, complete
with mountain folk values and barnyard menagerie.
An uncharted island in the South Pacific, a small rural
community complete with pet pigs within commut-
ing distance of New York? No problem at all. In fact,
the problems are eased, the plot is simplified. All that
is necessary now is a misdirected nose wiggle and the
boss is turned into a monkey.

The supporting character is caught directly in the
middle. Darren knows that his wife, his daughter, and
his mother-in-law are witches. He is surrounded by
"situation." There is no way for him to avoid involvement and the continued jarring of his sense of the
real. Finally, even he accepts the new order of reality
as we see him pleading that Samantha not give up
her powers in order to preserve their marriage. He
married her for what she is, he says, and that means
witchness along with everything else.

These supporting characters serve a crucial function
in that they stand, dramatically, closer to the value
structure of the audience than to that of the central
characters. Uncle Harry is a tightwad. He will not
give Lucy a raise, though he should know by now that
every refusal to do so will result in a scheme on her
part and that he will most likely suffer in the outcome.
His straightforward attitude precipitates an often
incoherent sequence of events. Similarly, Banker Drysdale of "The Beverly Hillbillies" stands in awe of both
the Clampetts' money and their value structure. Because he does not share their simplistic view of the
world, however, he cannot share their wealth, despite
his attempts to do so. But, then, very few people in
the audience are hillbillies, much less millionaires, and
cannot see the relationship between their world and
the "situation" that entertains them.

For the supporting characters and for the audience to whom they directly relate, the world of such situations is an amusing and frustrating one. It is an embarrassing sort of frustration because the audience always knows more than the characters involved and watches time after time as an innocent or not-so-innocent character walks into the trap of his or her own actions. If the situation comedy consisted solely of the antics of the characters, if we were repeatedly forced to involve ourselves merely in laughing at the pie-in-the-face aspects of the formula, it would remain at the level of embarrassment. But there is a recurring structure that outlines every episode of situation comedy, and that outline is ultimately the defining factor of the formula.

Lucy takes a fall and lodges her hand in a coffeepot just prior to serving at an exclusive social function. Gilligan swallows a radio that suddenly receives signals from a spacecraft. Jeannie, the genie, sends her husband to the base without his pants. How should a character behave under such circumstances? In many cases the stars of situation comedy avoid the most natural conclusion to such a sequence of events. Lucy, for example, never tells her hostess that a coffeepot is stuck on her wrist; Jeannie's husband never admits to having married a genie. For if natural solutions were sought, the stories could never exist. Finding contorted paths out of such inane thickets is precisely the business of situation comedy.   Action

The action involved will fall into four basic parts: the establishment of the "situation," the complication, the confusion that ensues, and the alleviation of the complication. The essential factor is the remedying of the confusion. It is rather like a mathematical process, the removing of parentheses within parentheses. In some cases it is accomplished merely by the explanation scene. In the Lucy episode that has served as our primary example, the entire show was given over to the creation of confusion in a single central scene which gave full play to the talents of the central characters. The clarification of that confusion was accomplished in a simple verbal explanation following the final commercial. In the episode of "Bewitched," however, in which the salesman was changed into a small boy, there was much more to do. In the attempt to clarify the physical elements of the confusion, more confusion followed. The removal of the spell was not an easy task, and time was spent demonstrating that the man's life would be seriously impaired by his nine-year-old body. In addition, the man learned the foolishness of wishing for a world of eternal childhood. But in both cases, the structure finally brings us full circle to a state of "normalcy."

Such "normalcy" is obviously "unreal." What does it mean to return to the normal state in which the witches are behaving like the good humans who surround them? Each of these shows is built on a complication that could never arise in "real" life. What, then, accounts for the success of such a formula? Why does it sell so well? What sense of need does this pattern tap so that it draws audience after audience, year after year? Clearly, though there is a sense of entertainment in the fantastic nature of some of the situations, and in the antics of the comic stars whom we enjoy watching, there is more than that, too. I would suggest that the more fundamental appeal of the situation comedy is found precisely in the fact that everything always "comes out all right."

What we see in the situation comedy is the establishment of a problem and an absolutely thorough solution to that problem. As suggested earlier, the audience always knows that the solution will be found. It is impossible that Lucy will be hurt by a scheming Bob, out to take advantage of her middle-aged dreams. It is impossible that the toy salesman will remain forever bewitched, an adult trapped unwillingly in a young boy's body. Rather, we know that all the parties involved will not only solve their problems but laugh at them, and laugh together, at each other. There is a warmth that emerges from the corrected mistakes, a sort of ultimate human companionship.

Such a feeling arises from the basic formula of human failure and human response. No one intends to cause pain in the shows, no one intends evil. The problems exist solely at the level of misunderstanding. Drysdale may desire the Clampetts' money, but he is not willing to steal and kill for it. Uncle Harry may not be free with salary raises, but he is quick to defend Lucy from emotional harm. So what if it is a one-sided world populated by characters totally innocent of our reality, or even if the characters are not of our order of reality at all? The possibility of the fantastic solution, of the magical paths out of our troubles, is a recurring human dream. And it is, as we observed in Chapter 1, one of the basic characteristics of popular art. The audience is reassured in its beliefs; it is not challenged by choice, by ambiguity, or by speculation about what might happen under other "realistic" circumstances. The character is not forced to examine his or her values, nor is the audience. In the situation comedy, there is no particular set of beliefs to be dealt with. There is only the barest, most basic outline, the paradigm. Human beings create problems for themselves; human beings resolve those problems, even in nonhuman situations. It is the upturned line of comedy in its barest form, and the result is a sigh of relief along with the laughter.

One need only recall the closing scenes of the old "Perry Mason" series to see that this outline is involved in a direct relationship with the rest of television. There, following the torturous solutions to murders, kidnappings, extortions, and intimidations, following the disintegration of criminals on the witness stand, we could always find Perry and Paul and Della and their clients, smiling over cigarettes and coffee, laughing at another case solved. In formulas other than situation comedy, however, the problems that our television stars must solve become more brutal. They also become more social and political in nature. Consequently, the values that are embodied in these formulas take on the same sort of specified, identifiable nature.

The closest step, however, is the most gentle. We move down the suburban streets and enter other homes where the humor is not quite so riotous and where the problems are a bit closer to those that most of us know. Those problems occur in the formula for domestic comedy.

The ritualistic, paradigmatic world of situation comedy is clearly antecedent to that of domestic comedy. Its dependence on people, on some sort of family setting, and on human error as the basis of plot structure offer many elements to its more "homey" counterpart. These similarities, however, rarely extend beyond the structural level, and there is a great difference in the mass of detail that defines the two forms. In a sense, the world of the situation comedy is much more tightly controlled than that of the domestic comedy because the insistence on the problem-solution outline forces each episode into a lockstep of regularity. Similarly, with character and event determined by formula, interaction among characters is minimized, and the result is a world that will not allow for changes or for development. There is simply no room for growth.

The domestic comedy, though restricted in other ways, is more expansive. There is less slapstick, less hysterical laughter. There is more warmth and a deeper sense of humanity. The cast built on the family as group is capable of reducing dependence on a single star, a single style. A richer variety of event, a consequent deepening of character, and a sense of seriousness enable the formula to build on the previous comic outline in significant ways.

The establishing shots in the various series introduce us immediately to the more physical aspects of these differences. In "The Lucy Show" and in "Bewitched" cast names and credits are run while cartoonized versions of the central characters mimic their human counterparts. The fantastic world of the situation comedy is defined by the fact that these characters are structurally "unreal," just as the cartoons are unreal. In "The Beverly Hillbillies" and "Gilligan's Island" opening songs recount in narrative form the events that lead up to the built-in situation on which each show is based.

The domestic comedy offers, by contrast, not an introduction to situation, but an introduction to setting. The camera follows Jim Anderson's car down a quiet street where houses are surrounded by large trees and picket fences. We turn with him into a driveway, and as he steps out of the car, we are introduced to the world of "Father Knows Best." A photograph of a large

frame house fades into reality, and we are welcomed
to the world of "My Three Sons." The camera picks
up a cowboy hat rising over a hill in yet another tree-
lined street, and we watch as Jimmy Stewart emerges,
riding a bicycle into the front yard of a large old
Victorian house, typical for the role of college professor he plays. We are "at home" in "The Jimmy Stewart Show."

What the producers have taken pains to establish is
a strong sense of "place." The houses we see are resi-
dential rather than suburban, found in small towns or
older, more established portions of cities. Here the
streets wind naturally, the sidewalks are neatly
trimmed. Even the variations bear out the pattern.
The family of "Family Affair" lives in a modern apartment building in New York. Care is taken, however,
in the opening shots to show us the outside of the
building and to locate it specifically adjacent to a
lovely city park. In "The Mary Tyler Moore Show" we
are treated to shots of an interstate highway, of
downtown Minneapolis' familiar landmarks, and of a
Victorian mansion remodeled to house several apartments.

Such settings, of course, are archetypically American. The use of older houses in small town settings is
a conscious attempt to build on a set of responses to
that pattern. The city park as surrogate lawn recalls
an older time when parks were considered the play
yards of the municipal family, visited as safely as one
would visit a neighbor's garden. Even for those of us
who do not experience such scenes daily they are a
part of our consciousnesses. They inform us of older
meanings, link us with a more familiar reality than
that provided by the situation comedy. The reality,

it turns out, may not be the one in which we live, but it is one that defines much of what we do.

Internally, the houses continue to reflect the rooted sense of reality begun outdoors. The sitcom interior was space that existed primarily for the purpose of the formula: it offered a setting in which things could happen. Such space needs no actual definition and could be a stage setting as well as a setting for a television program. The interior sets of the domestic comedy, however, are defined by the uses of the typical American family. Rooms are defined by function and by personality, used for certain purposes, commanded by certain individuals.

The kitchen, for example, is a special place. It is the domain of the mother, whose sex role is more stereotyped than that of the lead comedienne of the situation comedy. Whenever personal problems are taken to the kitchen, they are soon to be defined or solved in the softer, more "feminine" manner. Here, Mother counsels the children and nurses minor wounds. And when Father cannot sleep, we find him in the kitchen pouring a glass of milk. Mother will soon appear to prepare a midnight snack or to warm the milk.

The living room is most appropriately the room of the father, though in some cases there is also a den or an office that serves him. In the living room other members of the family are welcome, but Father relaxes here. The furnishings are more worn than those of the sitcom living room. Father can sit here in a favorite chair, waiting until an appropriate hour for daughter to return from her date. Past that hour he must go to the kitchen to worry.

Bedrooms are highly personal in nature and are defined by the individuals who occupy them. They are decorated in keeping with children's ages and occupations. The bedroom of the parents is more private, the area of important discussion. But privacy is a function of all bedrooms, and brothers and sisters do not violate the space of their siblings. Any number of plots may be generated from the theme of violated space, and ultimately any room in the house can be explored and exploited for its possibilities in creating plot.

Such possibilities are realized because the houses and rooms of domestic comedy, by contrast with those of situation comedy, are used. There is a sense of movement and activity there because by definition domestic comedy is dependent on people. Movement can begin as children rumble down the stairs for breakfast or as the father hurries out the door, late for work. It can begin as he enters the kitchen in the afternoon or as the children return from school. As a consequence of such movement, there is always a feeling of use about these sets, a sense of clutter that makes us aware of the ways they are lived in.

The movement enhances our sense of life most strongly by indicating the existence of a world outside the house. It is a world of offices for fathers, schools for children, and shops and clubs for Mother —the perfectly stereotyped pattern. In the situation comedy all such external factors would have to be connected in some way to the current situation or complication. There is no sense of going to work other than for purposes of finding out what will happen to the character. There is no way for the central character in a sitcom to enter a grocery store without precipitating some sort of comic action. The world of the domestic comedy is a world that creates, by contrast, the illusion of being lived in rather than acted in, and consequently there is a sense of involvement. To some degree it is this involvement that creates a seriousness even in the midst of exceptionally funny events.

These differences in setting, in the more physical aspects of the two formulas, are not meant to suggest that there are no direct relationships among them. Indeed, when we begin to translate out some of the significances of the setting, we see immediately that the two forms are directly related. Once again we find ourselves rooted firmly in the upper-middle class. With no outrageous variations designed to facilitate situations the sense of the average is, if anything, more pronounced. Again the homes are exceptionally comfortable. This is true in the emotional as well as in the physical sense, for there is always the feeling that the homes are long since paid for. There is no sense of brief tenure, of the transient family. The children are well-dressed and well-fed. If they do ask for something that the father cannot "afford," they are taught to work for it in the best middle-class manner.

The shift in meaning comes when we realize the importance of the greater emphasis on persons than on situations. We simply see more people. We see more of their homes and we see their toys, clothes, food, and other evidences of life. It is a matter of degree, of tone. The concern exhibited for Lucy by Kim and Uncle Harry is basically a family concern. Such concern could easily be the focus of a domestic comedy episode, though there is less likelihood of the extreme measures taken by Lucy's protectors. The prosperity and the personal emphasis indicate that this world is one of great stability. Such stability is grounded in part in possession and ownership.

In a much more important sense, however, the stability grows out of the family unit itself. Here are people who support each other, who share each other's problems and joys. The real basis for domestic comedy is a sense of deep personal love among the members of the family. Essential to such families is a sense of groupness, of interdependence. The interdependence is impossible without a strong sense of role definition. Members of families in domestic comedies know who they are. When there does occur some doubt, when a son challenges his father's wisdom or a daughter is unsure of her responses to a young man, we have the components for a plot conflict. The resolutions to such conflicts leave us with a stronger sense of the family as a unit in which the roles are redefined and re-established.

The father stands at the center of the family. In the most traditional sense he provides leadership and wisdom, and it is not so important that Father knows *best* as it is that Father *knows*. Much of his wisdom and authority rise from the fact that he has a much stronger definition of his function outside the home. In specific episodes the action centers on the role he plays in the home, but we are not allowed to forget that he is the provider and that he faces situations that require serious judgment throughout the day. Jim Anderson is, significantly, an insurance salesman. Other fathers may be engineers or government consultants. They must care for families other than their own, and in their professional capacity their ability to care and to decide is continually defined and tested.

Such men become centers of authority in their families because they are practiced in decision-making, in exercising their "power." Within the family, however, we consider them doubly wise because they never allow such authority to exceed the bounds of wisdom. They are rarely harsh in their judgments. They present familial justice tempered with much mercy. Essentially their role is that of adviser, and if it is at all possible, they much prefer allowing a member of the family to become aware of his or her own errors without resorting to explicit measures.

The role of the mother is in keeping with the cultural stereotype. She reassures us by acting as the provider of physical comforts within the home. Though she is not the primary judge of actions within the family, she is often the source of behind-the-scenes wisdom. She is the one who can point out to Father the folly of his initial decision. Her wisdom is increased by her choice to allow the father the appearance of superiority in his role, even though she has directed the decision.

The roles of children are equally well defined and depend heavily on standard, popular stereotypes for their content. Often they appear to have arrived fully defined from movies of the forties or fifties, even when they are updated in terms of dress or actions. Physically they must be in the process of "growing up." This is especially true for boys, though both sexes go through the pangs of sexual initiation and encounter, within the discreet bounds of what is permissible on TV, of course. The problems they face in all areas must eventually be turned over to the parents, who, in their wisdom, will solve them in the most gentle manner.

Small children occupy special places in these homes. They appear as dolls or toys, and they are always handled with care. Because they see the world from a different perspective, they often add to the action that takes place. Their view of the adolescent and adult worlds frequently reminds adolescents and adults of their shortcomings, and "out of the mouths of babes" is a frequent plot device. Ultimately their presence is almost always a tempering agent, and it is not uncommon for an episode to end with the delightful and perceptive remarks of a seven-year-old.

As in the situation comedy there are a variety of characters who play only incidental roles. One group of supporting characters, however, is much more important in domestic comedy than in situation comedy. These characters are not actual members of the family, but in many cases, especially when the family is not biologically complete, they fulfill surrogate family roles. Early domestic comedy offered its audiences exceptionally simple family groups. "The Life of Riley," "Ozzie and Harriet," and "Leave It to Beaver" bring us varying arrangements of siblings. Then followed a series of shows in which families seem to have suffered repeated patterns of loss. One of the parents was missing. In some later cases, these partial families find other partial families, and the result is a huge, multiple group such as "The Brady Bunch."

In the intervening period, however, it was necessary to replace the missing parent with some sort of substitute. In "Family Affair," Mr. French, the butler-maid-chef-jack-of-all-trades, fills the role of mother, offering a gentler, more indirect sort of influence than that offered by Uncle Bill, the authority figure for the show. The same role is filled by Mrs. Livingstone in "The Courtship of Eddie's Father," and here care is taken that she is both older and Oriental in order to preclude sexual interest on the part of the father. In a somewhat different vein, in "The Ghost and Mrs. Muir" the ghost of a long-dead sea captain acts as the authority figure for a fatherless family.

Such factors lead us to define the television "family" in rather nontraditional terms. Any group that is united by ties of love, of warmth, and of mutual concern can be termed a family. In almost every case the two major roles of the authoritative father and the counseling mother must be filled in some way. The essential factor is a set of shared values which define the "groupness" of the family. The growth of these ideas is crucial in developing a sense of probability for the show.

These extensions of the typical family make it possible for the concept of family to be developed even in units or groups in which there are no blood ties. One speaks, for example, of the "family" of "The Mary Tyler Moore Show." Mary, the star of the show, is clearly the central character. She portrays a single girl pursuing a career as a television associate producer. The supporting cast, however, rather than comprising a group of foils who serve only to highlight Mary's talents, performs familial functions. Rhoda, another single-working girl, lives in the same group of apartments in the remodeled house. She is much like a sister and is often found in Mary's apartment. She is also a parody of the Jewish mother, remembering her own mother's advice and making fun of it. Mary's boss, Lou Grant, is also a parody, of the authoritarian father. His rantings get him into more trouble than the conventional father, but he knows, finally, what he is talking about. Murray, Mary's colleague in the newsroom, is even-tempered and "realistic" in the manner of many television mothers. Ted Baxter, self-centered and comical anchor man for the evening news, suffers exactly the same conflicts and problems of an adolescent son. Much of what Mary does on the show resembles the sort of advisory problem-solving performed by fathers and mothers on the other shows. The group is tightly knit and the comic hostility that the members exhibit toward each other is based on an intergroup affection much like that of a traditional family. A number of episodes have explicitly explored these relationships, and a favorite theme deals with the fact that the most "disliked" member of the family, Ted, is really the most vulnerable and most in need of group protection. Clearly, the concept of family can extend to other members of the household who are not blood relations, to co-workers, or even to whole towns in which the cast is closely united by deep personal concern.

The complex family structures of domestic comedy generate innumerable problems on which to contrive plots. The problems build on the human failure syndrome we noted in the situation comedy, and the problem-solving paradigm carries directly into the other formulas. In the earlier form, however, the failures were centered in physical problems: mistaken identities, misplaced objects, physical mishaps, and so on. Though such problems also arise in domestic comedy, they establish far fewer of the plot structures than in sitcom. Here the problems are more likely to be mental and emotional. Failure takes place in the areas of complex human interaction, though the plots themselves could seldom be called complex. Because each member of the family plays a well-defined, highly stereotyped role, it is possible for any member of the family to become the center of an individual episode. The extended family thus serves the function of allowing action and emphasis to be spread among larger numbers of individuals. This, too, contrasts with situation comedy in which our attention is continually drawn back to the star.

Paralleling this change in the nature of the problems is a change in the manner of resolving problems. While it is true that the outcome is never in doubt, that the problem will be resolved in a manner that will release the built-up tension, it is also true that there is more room for ambiguity and complexity, admittedly of a minimal sort. Characters do seem to change because of what happens to them in the problem-solving process. Usually they "learn" something about human nature.

This learning process is directed toward three major groups. If the problem has something to do with the terrors and trials of "growing up," it is likely that the lesson will be directed toward one of the children. If the problem is directed toward a broader concept and the lesson has to do with human nature in general, the learner will probably be an adult. Frequently, the adult, in the course of guiding the child through a problem, will learn a general truth and both functions will be served in the same involvement. More importantly, however, is the way in which the audience learns. This learning process is enhanced by many of the physical details we have noted. It is largely for this reason that we have been treated to outside views of houses and to living rooms that are cluttered instead of the sterile interiors of sitcom. If the wife of the family burns the dinner or the child seems brokenhearted over the loss of a toy, the world seems somehow closer to our own, and with the lessened distinction between the two worlds the morals of domestic comedy become direct statements to the audience.

One of Mary Tyler Moore's neighbors desperately asks that Mary inform her ten-year-old daughter of the facts of life. When all the contortions are completed, when Mary sits down with the girl and begins her speech, the child informs her that she knows all about *that* from biology class. What she really needs

to know about is "love." Mary has learned how to deal
with the child, and her advice directs the girl toward
her own self-discovery of love. The audience has
been reassured that there is still a distinction between
sex and love, that old notions still prevail.

In a similar episode of "The Jimmy Stewart Show"
we are confronted with the apparently simple problem that Father needs a new briefcase. Everyone in
the family decides, without group consultation, to buy
one for his birthday. His wife goes to the local luggage
shop and selects a sealskin case which, unfortunately,
costs over a hundred dollars. She settles for a more
utilitarian model. The older son, after much thought
and discussion with his wife, buys the expensive
model. The close friend of the family buys a handsome attaché case. All of the gifts are presented at
the same time and with various expressions of great
love and respect. The older son points out that his
expense has been small return for what he has received from his father. The friend fumbles for words
of affection. The wife acknowledges her continuing
love. Finally, though, all of the cases are stored away.
The favored gift comes from the very young son who
has sewed a book bag from cloth given to him by his
mother. Because of the deeply personal concern, his
own handicraft, the father chooses to honor this gift,
and he explains this to the family.

He also explains it to the audience. His actions and
statements to his family during the events of the episode make clear to the audience the values of love
and support that we discussed earlier. But "The Jimmy
Stewart Show" does not let the comment rest with
such indirect presentation. Making explicit what is
implied in all the domestic comedies, Stewart ad-
dresses the audience directly at the end of each

show. It is difficult to tell whether or not he speaks as his character or as Jimmy Stewart. Indeed, the two "people" are woven tightly together. In either case, he speaks to "us," without the fictional frame of the show. Each week he comments on the outcome of the episode and then concludes by telling us that he and his family wish each of us and our family "peace, love, and laughter."

These concepts—peace, love, and laughter—are the central virtues of the world of the domestic comedy. In the situation comedy there is much laughter, there is a form of love, and there is very little peace of the sort indicated here. The domestic comedy is filled with such peace. It grows out of the love, and in the context of these two we discover a gentler form of laughter.

These values are grounded in the belief in the family as a supportive group. Within the family strength abides. The strength grows out of the mutual support that each of the family members is willing to offer and for which he or she receives like support in return. Many episodes are built on the minor ways in which family members hurt one another, sometimes consciously, sometimes not. With each resolution of such a problem, however, the family unit is strengthened. The group is the sheltering unit, particularly when we are made aware of the difficulties of the world surrounding the family.

Such support is grounded on the mutual respect of individuals. Any episode may be built on problems of privacy rights in the home, on problems with bullies and exploiters at school, and on all the problems rising from sibling rivalry, reinforcing the idea that the individual is the unit on which families are built.

The first to recognize these factors and the most

able at articulating solutions to most of them is the
father, or the authority center of the group. The wisdom of the father, with assists from the mother, is the
prime value asserted by the structures of domestic
comedy. This is not to suggest a value placed on
domination or authoritarianism. Quite the contrary,
such wisdom is strongest as an expression of that sense
of group warmth and support. The father speaks from
age and experience; his concern is to guide his children through problems so that they will learn from
their errors but not be destroyed by them. In most
cases it is the father who, by his actions or by his
direct explanation of what has happened, points the
moral that we take from domestic comedy.

Once again we must remember that such morals
and the values they reflect are the morals and values
of an older time. The white frame houses with picket
fences, the spreading, sheltering trees, and the flower
gardens mirror a time when families did not move
about the country several times during their lives.
They remind us of times when uncles and grandpar-
ents lived with their children and grandchildren. They
recall the possibility of young men entering their
fathers' businesses. In a sense the structures of domestic comedy form a world more like that of the nineteenth or early twentieth centuries than that of
present-day America.

What is important here is that we know that the
nineteenth or early twentieth centuries were not so
thoroughly warm and tender. But those years are far
enough removed from our present experience to be
cloaked in an ideal obscurity. This television version
of the past, when things were simpler and when order
was more prevalent than chaos, becomes more and
more crucial as we examine other forms of television

drama. The use of history to express another set of values becomes a major device in the creation of various forms.

This is not to say that those values—peace, love, and laughter—are outdated, or that they are no longer present in America. On the contrary, they are among the old verities. The problem arises when we compare their expression in the domestic world of television's happy homes with their expression in our own world. Domestic comedy may not be untrue, but it is unfinished. No matter how serious the problem, no matter how critical the conflict faced by the child, the problem will emerge as solved. This factor remains constant from situation to domestic comedy. There remains the magic of the wise father, the counseling mother, the obedient child. The sense of completeness, of the happy ending, is the popularity factor. Yet one is left with the image of fathers and mothers delighting in the antics of "My Three Sons" while they are slightly unsure of the whereabouts of their own children.

The deep cultural appeal of this form is made clear when we realize that the most significant innovations in television rise from it. When the problems encountered by the families become socially or politically significant, this form can be expanded. The frame of the ordered world is shattered. Families find themselves living in the world of the present without magical solutions and, to some extent, without the aid of peaceful and laughing love. Comedy, in the form of "All in the Family" or "Maude" or "M*A*S*H," is changed into the perfect vehicle for biting social commentary. Clearly this has long been the case with traditional comic forms: from Aeschylus to Chaplin artists have recognized this power. For television,

however, the sense of satire and commentary was long
in coming. When it did begin to present answers that
were not totally acceptable at the mass cultural level,
a new stage had been reached. In the meantime, other
forms and formulas applied the same sort of acceptable
answers to larger and more crucial social problems
which became, without question, the content of the
more action-oriented series.

3

WESTERNS: THE TELEVISION VERSION

In an important sense the formulas of the situation and domestic comedy are the creation of television. There are antecedents, of course, in popular literature, in farce, melodrama, vaudeville, and the movies. But the rigid patterns of a narrative frame involving families, problems, solutions, and specific social attitudes in a comic outline have developed in the television years into a major form of mass entertainment. This is not the case with the Western or the mystery. These forms have long since been repeatedly defined in literary, dramatic, and cinematic representations, and their roots may be traced to Cooper, Scott, Poe, even to Sophocles. More importantly, these are the forms that have provided, since the middle of the nineteenth century, mass entertainment for large segments of the American audience. In adapting such forms for television the producers assured themselves of a ready-made audience, and even though the relative popularity of any one of the forms may at times exceed that of the others, there has never been a time when some representative of each of them did not appear in regular television programming.

In a way these forms stand at the center of popular art; they are the ones first thought of when discussions of popular culture begin. This is due to their historical development, but it is even more the result of the special nature of the worlds created by Westerns and mysteries. These worlds depend on basic human reactions to elements of adventure, excitement, tension, and resolution. Here we witness the uses of violence, the variations developed on themes of death, trials, tests, and examinations of physical and moral strength. We also find worlds that have carefully and completely defined value systems, where characters and audience are caught in a complex of expectations which must be worked out satisfactorily. If these expectations are violated, if the patterns are broken or remain incomplete, it is quite likely that we are no longer in the realm of popular art, but are moving into areas in which large portions of the audience will experience some sort of discomfort.

No one is more aware of these defining elements than the television producers. Their understanding of the basic formulaic elements of the classical popular entertainments was demonstrated in the American Broadcasting Corporation's special program saluting television's twenty-fifth year of national programming. Their tribute to the bread-and-butter Western and mystery forms came in the fashion of two musical production numbers. In the first version we are introduced to an abstraction of the Western setting. On the street of a "western town" no pretense is made to disguise the cardboard setting: a saloon, a jail, a store. A narrator informs us that the villain who owns the saloon also controls the town, and we are simultaneously introduced to the typical black-clad character. Next comes the hero; dressed completely in white, he rides a live white horse onto the abstract set. No one knows who he is or where he has come from, and as he walks into the saloon, several groups of interested loungers follow him through the swinging doors. The interior of the saloon is in keeping with the out-

door set. A balcony, a bar, and several poker tables
define it for the viewer. The hero and the villain clash
initially over one of the bar girls, but before they fight
seriously, the "star" of the saloon girls appears on the
balcony, and it is clear that she and the hero are taken
with one another, a bad omen. A poker game begins
and the hero soon discovers that the villain is cheat-
ing. In the ensuing fistfight the hero knocks out the
villain and prepares to leave the town. The villain
follows him into the street and is about to shoot him
in the back, but the girl runs between them and is
killed. The hero then shoots the villain, mounts his
horse, and rides away. The narrator closes the segment by informing us that the characters in this
"tragedy" are never forgotten. Rather, the story becomes legend, part of the folklore and history of the
town.

Other than the narration there has been no dialogue.
No attempt has been made to create characters, to
"develop" action. The entire number was danced in a
highly stylized manner. But it was clearly a Western.
There could have been no doubt in the mind of the
audience that the pattern played out there had been
played out thousands of times before, in novels, plays,
movies, and television shows. The mixture of fantasy
and reality, the live horse in the center of an abstract
design, cuts to the central factor in the idea of popular entertainment through which the audience remains in its own world while "living" in the other of
violent extremes and powerful action. This is the West
at its most archetypal level, the triumph of good over
evil, the establishment of order in the unformed frontier town. The death of the saloon girl becomes symbolic of the bittersweet acceptance of order in place

of the freedom offered in the rawness of the settle-ment.

A half hour later the formula was repeated, iden-tical on the level of action, totally shifted in terms of history and environment. The setting has now become a fog-covered harbor area, the villain a gangster who controls the criminal action of the docks. The hero ar-rives in a glistening white Corvette. The saloon has been transformed into a sleazy waterfront bar, and the saloon girl is explicitly identified as a prostitute. The outcome of the action, of course, is the same.

Such abstractions ignore crucial differences between Westerns and mysteries. Although they do define some common elements that might account for the almost universal appeal of these formulas, they overlook the cultural shifts that help to account for different au-diences, different attitudes toward entertainment, and basically different responses to the art forms. If the anniversary show had allowed the dance numbers to pass as the only statement regarding these two central elements in the world of television, the com-ment would have been very insufficient. But there were other features which, though they were not planned as formal recognition of the Western and the mystery, gave the audience a more complex defini-tion of the meaning of television entertainment.

While presenting a special award to James Arness, the star of "Gunsmoke," John Wayne offered his definition of the "adult Western." In a pure Western, he suggested, the problems are solved by shooting the villain; in the adult Western problems are solved by talking the villain to death. A humorous distinction, to be sure, at least in John Wayne's eyes, but the dis-tinction becomes important in defining the television Western. In a similar moment Efrem Zimbalist, Jr., star of "The FBI," informed the audience that law and order had reigned for twenty-five years in America—at least on television. Such a comment has overwhelming cultural importance in the study of television mystery shows. Perhaps the most telling moment came when Lorne Greene accepted a special award for "Bonanza." The recognition, he suggested, was marred for him and for much of the audience by the fact that Dan Blocker, one of his costars, had died unexpectedly only a few months before the celebration. As Hoss Cartwright, Blocker had become for many people the most popular member of the "Bonanza" family, the definitive expression of the television cowboy.

These three comments, seen in conjunction with the production numbers, begin to suggest some of the complexity involved in a study of television's artistic qualities, especially when those qualities are expressed in forms adapted from the familiar patterns of entertainment common to American culture. As Wayne makes clear, those forms are changed by television. Zimbalist goes further, facetiously suggesting that the world of television is concerned with the issues critical to our own world of experience and hinting that TV's world can become a substitute for our own. Greene deals with our difficulty in distinguishing between characters and the performers who portray them, and calls us to sadness for the fate of "Bonanza" as well as for Blocker. These problems are made even more difficult when the entertainment forms are directly related to history and environment as these are. The Western and the mystery grow out of definable cultural moments, adapting and commenting on these factors in the creation of popular art.

Television adds a special complexity in creating its own versions of these forms.

The viewer of the television Western, for example, shares many of the delights that the audience of the popular Western has always had available. He or she knows, for instance, that at least some of the places and people who figure in these "fictions" were real. Bat Masterson, Wyatt Earp, Daniel Boone, Boonesboro, Dodge City, Tombstone: these are names that emerge from historical reality. Even when the specific events, characters, and places are not real, we know that they emerge from historical moments and actual types. There was indeed a "real" West, with cowboys and Indians, saloon girls and rustlers, range wars, brush fires, and cattle drives. In addition to these factors, however, is the even richer world of "the Western," the form familiar to us in books, movies, radio, and comics. That West is exempt from history, is able somehow to remain the same forever, richer for its legendary, "untrue" additions than factual history can ever be. Which West is the "real" one for most people? Which has had the most influence on our lives, on our national image, on politics and foreign policy?

But beyond these two factors is a third element in the mix which is peculiar to television, to American culture of the past twenty-five years. That factor has to do with our familiarity with the world of the television Western series, the "reality" of "Gunsmoke" itself. People exist there whom we have come to know intimately. Marshal Dillon, Doc, Kitty, Chester/Festus, and the town regulars are people whom we recognize, people about whom we care. They have taken on an existence that goes far beyond their fictional characterization. When Milburn Stone suffers a heart attack, Doc Adams, the character he portrays, receives thousands of letters wishing him well. For whom are the letters intended? Or, in a more potent example, we may ask who died suddenly in 1972, Dan Blocker or Hoss Cartwright? The question is all the more important when we realize that Hoss's death has been written into the show. In spite of that, Hoss will continue to be seen in reruns for years to come so that some viewers will doubtless fail to recognize that the "real" person no longer exists.

What this suggests is that television is creating another world for us, continuous and familiar, inevitably available for anyone who wishes to be entertained. If we desire gentle amusement, some good fun and warmth after dinner, we can view the situation-domestic comedy. But if we desire excitement and adventure, a somewhat harsher world, we can turn to the world of the Western or the mystery. Even so, however, television's worlds are not so distinct. The crucial point is that in adapting the clearly recognizable forms of popular entertainment for its own uses, some of the distinctions begin to fade, and the forms are changed into specifically television versions of themselves. Those versions often bear more resemblance to each other than to their nontelevision counterparts. Recent television Westerns are directly related to recent mysteries and both bear strong resemblance to the formulas we have already discussed, the situation and domestic comedy. For the world of television is a world of explicit values, and in the evolution of forms we see more and more how values from one segment of that world filter into other segments, and ultimately into our own lives.

The West of the popular arts is a familiar place to almost every American, regardless of whether or not he or she currently happens to be a fan of one of the expressions of that art. At some time all of us have come into contact with the West. We have seen the movies, perhaps read the novels and magazines and comics, have watched the television. So have critics, historians, and psychologists and sociologists. The Western and the mystery have been analyzed more thoroughly than most of the popular art formulas, with the result that the major elements of the formulas are available and familiar.

The first crucial elements in defining the Western are time and place. Rarely has such a brief episode in American history had such cultural impact as in the case of the "frontier West." For less than fifty years there was something that resembled the popular Western. The characters were created there not in actuality, but in conception and events took place there that gave rise to legend. Attitudes may have been expressed that were expanded into codes. But the conceptualization, the creation of legend, and the expansion of attitudes took place somewhere else, in the creations of the popular arts. As a result the time and place of the West are frozen into American consciousness. Regardless of whether or not such characters, events, and attitudes ever existed in actual experience, they now exist in the art and have for nearly a century. The place remains because it gave rise to certain events that have come to have meaning far beyond historical reality. Time remains because events are honored and allowed, by contrast with "real" time, in which they are prohibited by law and by custom.

We know that we are in a Western, then, if we recognize the American frontier setting and place it between 1860 and some time progressing into the first decade of the twentieth century. It may have a spe-

cific location such as Texas or Kansas, but it may be
an abstraction, a composite of all the other Westerns
that we know of and have experienced. We must have
plains or badlands or deserts or mountains. We must
have men on horseback or in wagons. The towns must
be unfinished, rugged, expressive of a sort of raw
newness. Both literary and visual forms use and define our sense of this environment, and it is not accidental that NBC introduced color programming on a
regular basis with the "Bonanza" series.

To a certain extent these factors are important in
themselves, offering a glance backward, a sense of
historical continuity for the national experience, and
an examination of a relatively unspoiled landscape.
Certainly those elements contribute to the special appeal of the Western as formula. But the factors are
even more important because they define the time and
place in which certain types of events were possible.
In this respect the Western and the mystery fulfill one
of the basic formulaic needs for television art. Once
again we see the use of the problem paradigm, so
well defined in the sitcom. Here the problems were
built in prior to the video adaptations.

The frontier setting and the physical environment
of the West define a specific problem that must be
solved if the Western is to be truly representative of
its formula. The central problem for the Western is
the establishment of order, the bringing of civilization. It is within this framework that the numerous
Western plots might be developed, each of which offers a variation on the problem of order versus savagery. Frank Gruber suggests seven basic Western
plots which encompass the central Western theme.

1) The Union Pacific Story centering around the
construction of a railroad, telegraph or stagecoach

line or around the adventures of a wagon train;
2) The Ranch Story with its focus on conflicts
between ranchers and rustlers or cattlemen and
sheepmen; 3) The Empire Story, which is an epic
version of the Ranch Story; 4) The Revenge Story;
5) Custer's Last Stand, or the Cavalry and Indian
Story; 6) The Outlaw Story; and 7) The Marshal
Story. [Quoted in John Cawelti, *The Six-Gun
Mystique* (Bowling Green, Ohio, 1970), pp. 34–35]

In each of these stories civilization is pitted against
savagery, and this struggle leads to the third major
factor, the action of the characters.

The Western hero is the man who brings order. He
may be an Indian fighter, a marshal, a cavalry officer,
a gunfighter, or a wagon master. Unlike the helpless
townspeople or untrained immigrants from peaceful
Ohio, he possesses the proper skills with which to
cope with the threats of savagery. Indeed, he is necessarily tainted with savagery himself; he is able to bear
arms and willing to use them. At the end of the action
he may ride off into the sunset, return to his post or
his lonely office, marry the school mistress, or buy a
small ranch and join the townspeople. In any case he
has established authority, and the frontier in its most
basic form no longer exists where he operates, but is
extended a few miles farther to some other raw settle-
ment. This place, where the hero is, has become tame
by comparison. To a degree, then, this formula resembles those of the situation and domestic comedy, the
Western hero serving as an authoritative father figure,
replacing the gentle problem-solver of those other
forms. At this level the comparison is so distant as to
seem absurd.

The "meaning" of this formulaic action brings the
forms closer together. In a thorough study of the

Western formula Cawelti carefully suggests that the cultural implications of the Western might be related to the cultural position of adolescents, and that the Western might express "the conflict between the adolescent's desire to be an adult and his fear and hesitation about the nature of adulthood." Westerns, "through their legitimate violence . . . express the fear and hostility toward adults and the desire to punish them for their corruption which adolescents, at least until the current generation, have not found it easy to express directly." On the adult level,

it seems safe to conclude that the same psychological dynamic of hostility and fear of society mixed with an inability to recognize this aggressive anger for what it is can be, at least at times, a source of tension. . . . Particularly in a culture where social values are so confused and ambiguous about the relation between the individual and society, where some values place a great emphasis on individual aggressiveness and others emphasize social responsibility and conformity, the fantasy of the hero who reluctantly, but nobly aids the cause of social order by acts of individual violence probably corresponds to a widespread fantasy of legitimated aggression. [Ibid., pp. 83–84]

Cawelti reminds us that any such singly focused interpretation cannot account for the rich variety of form and content that can be found in the Western. For the viewer of television Westerns, however, such an interpretation sounds very familiar. For in that highly repetitive medium successful versions of the formulaic constructions are immediately copied in hopes that the success has tapped a rich vein of audience interest, conscious or unconscious. As we examine some of the changes in TV Western formats, we can note an increasing concern for the type of problem that gives full expression to the interpretation offered by Cawelti. Even more importantly, we will note a shifting version of that interpretation which not only provides for the expression of such a fantasy but offers a particular solution to the problem that lies at the center of it.

The Western in its simplest form arrived with the earliest television, and many literary and cinematic characters simply re-created their roles in the new medium. Roy Rogers, Hopalong Cassidy, the Lone Ranger, the Cisco Kid, and others immediately began to develop new juvenile audiences. On the more adult level we know the number of shows continued to grow throughout the fifties and into the early sixties. Warner Brothers entered the telefilm industry with "Cheyenne" in 1955 and followed its success with a series of imitators: "Sugarfoot," "Colt .45," "Bronco," and "Maverick" all duplicated the patterns and, in varying degree, the success of "Cheyenne." These programs depended on the clearest form of western involvement. The hero confronted the problem of the bad man and overcame him. The bad man, of course, took many forms, and the adventures of Cheyenne and his imitators involved them with cattle rustlers, renegade Indians, thieves, corrupt army officials or Indian agents, and so on through the list of antagonists found in any frontier setting. Each central character developed his unique personality, his own way of dealing with the problems, and his own characterization setting him apart from other Western heroes. Such differentiation was necessary, because the shows were series, dependent not on the ever-changing character of an archetypal Westerner, but on the ever-present, familiar star. Because he could not be killed, because the audience knew that he would return, he must be distinguished from the "star" who would be seen the following evening. Thus, Clint Walker became Cheyenne. And if there were no scene in which he could remove his shirt and exhibit the splendid Walker/Cheyenne torso, it might not really be an episode of "Cheyenne."

Within this standard Western/action format there was little room for the exploration of complex problems, the moral and social issues that might have been included on the frontier. A few shows attempted some sort of moral complexity, but even in series such as "Wanted—Dead or Alive" (Steve McQueen's highly successful show), in which we confronted the morally ambiguous position of the bounty hunter in episode after episode, it was the "white hat syndrome" that prevailed. Nowhere was this more obvious than in the "historical" shows which pretended to use actual historical figures for their central characters. Wyatt Earp and Bat Masterson, as they were depicted on television, bore little resemblance to the figures who can be reconstructed from historical sources, and the shows of the same name were among the most simple of all Westerns.

The same year that saw the introduction of "Cheyenne," however, also saw the beginning of "Gunsmoke," the most successful TV Western and one of television's great all-time successes. "Gunsmoke" was moved directly from radio, complete with theme song and an easily identifiable cast of characters. If "Cheyenne" had been a cut above the juvenile Western in creating mass adult entertainment, "Gunsmoke" moved a step further, billing itself from the start as an "adult" Western. The opening scene set the tone for the show. To a background of tense, pounding chords, Marshal Matt Dillon stepped into the street of Dodge City, Kansas. He faced another man in the classical shoot-out stance. Before the guns were drawn the camera cut to the face of the marshal, and there, week after week, we could easily see the flicker of anguish, the moral doubt–moral necessity involved in what he was about to do.

Then, from behind the marshal we saw the guns drawn, the shots fired. Down the street the opponent fell, shot dead. Dominating the entire sequence was the body of Matt Dillon, and in the final seconds of the shot we saw only his back, slightly hunched in the position of the fastest of the fast-draw experts. The dominance of his figure, the length of the street, the moment of doubt, the figure of the falling man —all these spoke of a harsher, more "realistic" West. Somehow, even though we knew that Matt Dillon could no more be killed than the Lone Ranger, there was something more serious about the whole matter, and we returned week after week to examine this world more closely.

The world of Dodge City is little more than a crossroads, and the sense of isolation is highly developed. "Somewhere" there are the other famous cities of the Kansas frontier: Hayes, Abilene. But we are willing to accept the illusion of reality that they can be reached only after a ride of days or even weeks. Around Dodge are the small farms and embryonic ranches. Far to the south is Texas, with its baronial cattle empires. The crossroads is the focal point and it is there that our attention is developed. Rarely does an episode take us out of the town, but in place of such travel we are regularly treated to wandering mountain men, trappers, wild-eyed and whiskey-starved drovers, the shapeless wives and urchin children of busted-out farmers who come from the surrounding area. We are made to care for these people. These are the ones for whom the frontier is a place of ultimate freedom, where people will succeed or fail. And we know when the plot begins that the frightened farmer who is staking his last smooth coin and worn bill on a poker hand is out of his element and likely to die, leaving the town with yet another widow and orphan family to be boarded at Ma Smalley's until money comes to pay for passage back to Indiana. We also know, however, that the man who kills the farmer, no matter how justified in this instance, must answer at some point to the moral superiority of Matt Dillon.

Dillon, Kitty, Doc, Festus, and a few minor characters stand as the perpetual agent/observers in the changing world of Dodge City. Their values define the standard by which other characters must be judged and instructed. The distinction between "Gunsmoke" and the more simplistic Western such as "Cheyenne" has to do with the ambiguity of those values. As indicated above, Matt Dillon is a man who does not like to resort to killing. At the same time he is thoroughly committed to the ideas of justice and order. He frequently cites the fact that he is a United States marshal and that his allegiance to the national government is much larger than that offered by the city of Dodge or the state of Kansas. He is the ultimate expression of the movement of civilization, of law, and if he must step into the street to kill, it is as that representative figure, often at odds with his own human response to the actions.

The ambiguous nature of these judgments is also developed in the relationships among the major characters. It should be clear to any viewer that Miss Kitty and Marshal Dillon are the principals in a long-standing affair. The fact that Kitty is the proprietress of a saloon makes her moral position in the community even more unclear, though the rawness of the frontier minimizes somewhat the conventional moral structures of the time. In spite of these factors, however, these characters will stand as the moral judges of the actions that surround them. They are the ones who are unwilling to make simplistic condemnations of other people's actions. In short, they are the representatives of sophistication and civilization just as Matt Dillon is the representative of the more legalistic aspects of order. As in any complex Western it is the combination of these factors that represents the true establishment of civilization. Justice tempered with mercy, morality tempered with humanity, these are the marks of the growing maturity of the town. Developing with that maturity is a shifting focus away from the classical problems of the western frontier toward the more human and individualistic aspects of those problems. If an aging mountain man roars into Dodge shooting windows out of saloons, we are more likely to get a psychological analysis of the meaning of a passing era than the quick solution of a gun butt to the back of the head, though that action might still play a crucial role in the analysis. These problems grow more and more specific and are reflected in the development of still other types of Westerns.

Psychological emphasis and western action found an almost perfect mix in the character of Paladin, central figure in the highly popular "Have Gun—Will Travel." Here the character exhibits both sides of the "modern" Western hero. Surrounded by beautiful women, Paladin spends much of his time at the chessboards and dining tables of the posh San Francisco hotel where he lives. Enamored of the finer things, he dines with the flair of the connoisseur. Throughout the rugged land of the Southwest, however, newspapers carry his advertisement, "Have Gun—Will Travel, Wire Paladin, San Francisco." When such a request arrives, he changes costumes and characteristics. Dressed totally in black, he travels to the source of the cry for help and performs whatever services may be needed. Such service usually requires violent action, at which Paladin is as expert as he is at the choice of the proper wine. Increasingly in the action of "Have Gun" Paladin is called on to solve the psychological and emotional problems of his clients as he resolves their more physical conflicts, a trend that has been adopted by many other forms as well as by other Westerns.

The most successful marriage of these two major attitudes of the television Western came in 1959 with the introduction of "Bonanza." It is difficult to say what the appeal of the program is, other than that it offers a special vision of America within the Western's central American image. With "Bonanza" the West and the Western become the province of those other crucial television factors—families and fathers. It is true, of course, that "Gunsmoke" has developed its own sense of family over the years, but with "Bonanza" this structure is expressed as the show's defining characteristic. It takes one of the central patterns of the Western formula, the cattle empire story, and fills it with the elements of family and psychology common to the more domestic types of television.

From the beginning "Bonanza" was one of those special, single-parent television families. Ben Cartwright fathered his three sons by different wives, outlived all the women, and was presented to the television audience with the robust young men who constituted his total family: Adam, the oldest, most nearly like his father, level-headed, sound, cool, representative of authority when Ben was not available; Hoss, the middle son, huge and comic, somewhat simple-minded, though infinitely shrewd when shrewdness became necessary; Little Joe, the youngest, hot-headed, dashingly handsome, too quick with his answers to violence. The three sons among them constituted a single, multifaceted individual character. But the model for the rounded, complete character was always before these young men in the figure of their father.

The Ben Cartwright figure is common to western lore as the empire maker: the taker of wives, the tamer of the land, the entrepreneur owner of silver mines, timberland, massive cattle herds. He is an authority figure not only with his own family but with the larger family of the community as well. Indeed, Virginia City, the historically physical touchstone of the show, seems to be the village at the edge of the empire, the tiny street over which towers the baronial vision of the Ponderosa. Ben exhibits the qualities of the Western hero in his strength, his coolness, his unwillingness to use violence, and his recognition that such use is a necessary part of his way of life. When it comes, it comes with devastating ability. To this degree he is very similar to Matt Dillon or to Paladin and to any number of literary and cinematic Westerners. In such a role Ben led his sons, in the early days of "Bonanza," into situations typical to Westerns. Much time, thought, and physical effort were given over to the defense of the Ponderosa from wandering outlaws and other characters who threatened the empire. The conflicts were essentially those of the classical Western.

But Ben was always something more than a Western hero, and as the other aspects of his role began to dominate, so the content of the show began to shift. Most importantly, Ben is not the lone hand, the solitary gunman, the isolated marshal, who must assume responsibility on the weight of moral or legal authority. He is a family man, and the values of family preservation are as strong for him as they are for Jim Anderson, of "Father Knows Best." Indeed, "Bonanza" can be seen as a more complex, harsher version of that show as well as a traditional Western. In this fatherly role Ben is highly conscious of serving as a model for his sons, of guiding them to make the right decisions. He is something less than authoritative and something more than permissive, unless a specific situation calls for the extreme in either case. He fosters among his sons the virtues of careful thought and analysis, of interdependence within the family and in society, of an abhorrence of gratuitous violence, and of the ultimate acceptance of responsibility which might call for violence in special situations.

Such a role is transcendent. It takes the traditional character from the popular art form and molds it into something immediately and directly related to contemporary society. The Western grasps the mass audience with its familiar patterns of conflict, but as a new form "Bonanza" offers that audience the particular cultural orientation of domestic comedy. In this way problems, conflicts, and issues that have nothing in particular to do with the classical Western can be viewed in a Western context. As a consequence, the Western can now be seen as directly related to the forms we have discussed. There we have seen that the determining values of domestic comedy are the values of an older time, that even when faced with a peculiarly contemporary situation the father-counselors of that world solve the problem with an argument for love or gentleness or compassion that might strike the typical viewer as somewhat simplistic. By using the Western as a vehicle, problems of the same sort may be raised to the social as opposed to the individual level. Answers are seen here as naturally simple, for the West of popular entertainment is a world of clear-cut values and strong beliefs. From the other point of view, when Westerners are faced with problems and issues that reflect contemporary society, their responses become somewhat more complicated. The television Western is no longer a simple-minded shoot-'em-up in which the rope and the gun solve social problems, nor is it the gentle world of the domestic comedy in which problems never seem to have social consequences. This complex function is clear in a recent installment of "Gunsmoke," a program which has developed more and more in the "Bonanza" vein by offering domestic sentimentality instead of traditional Western conflict.

The episode opens as a humble farmer is refused a loan by a refined and professional banker. As the farmer rejoins his wife, explaining that somehow they will get by, the bank is robbed. In passing, the chief of the robbers, a noted Robin Hood type, drops a large bill in the farmer's lap. Nevertheless, the farmer joins the posse in pursuit of the robbers. He is a comic figure, riding a plow horse that falls continually behind the other riders. Finally, lost and somewhat bewildered, he stumbles onto a cabin in which the head thief is hiding with one of his wounded men. The robber hears the farmer approach and moves for his gun. The farmer shuts his eyes, points his gun through a window, and shoots six times into the cabin. Both men in the cabin are killed, shot, it turns out, in the back. There are murmurings within the posse and these turn to open criticism as the townsmen argue that it is simply not right to shoot any man in the back. The farmer suffers internally for his deed, for he has never killed before. He also suffers the scorn of the town, though Festus, Doc, and Miss Kitty continually point out that the people are being foolish in condemning the man who performed a necessary and legal act. Nevertheless, the farmer is severely beaten by a group of townsmen, hooded to protect their identity. He knows who they are, but refuses to identify them and as a result is repeatedly ridiculed and persecuted. Even the banker whose money he saved refuses to reconsider the loan, fearing the public response to such a conciliatory act. The worst of the actions fall on the man's daughter. She is ridiculed at school by the other children. Her teacher, in response to the father's pleas for help, will not become personally involved. Finally, some of the townsmen hang the young girl's pet cat, and in a rage the farmer goes to town and begins to fight the bullies. Marshal Dillon goes to his aid and the two of them beat the entire group of toughs responsible for most of the persecution. In the final scene the family is packing to leave the area, hoping to use some reward money to start a new life elsewhere. But at the last moment the schoolteacher, having reconsidered his responsibility in the community and his example with the children, drives a wagon full of children to the farm. The children plead with the farmer and his family to stay and make their home in the community. In a final act of kindness they give the girl a new kitten. The audience knows at this point that all is well.

It should be noted that there have been a few minutes of the episode devoted to what could be called traditional western action. There was a bank robbery; the robber was a Robin Hood type; the posse did take up the chase that ended as the farmer killed with his six-gun. Even those scenes were largely undercut, however, by comic portrayal. The farmer with his wandering plow horse and dilapidated pistol are thoroughly laughable. The comedy culminates in the scene in which the farmer, eyes tightly shut, extends the pistol far from him and blazes away until the gun is empty. If anything he is the parody of the gunfighter.

Beyond this the story is not at all concerned with western action. Rather, the primary thematic concern of the episode has to do with the problem of irrational intolerance. In pursuing such a theme, of course, the code of the West is explicitly questioned, as Doc and Kitty and Festus argue against the nonsensical position of the townsmen who condemn the farmer as a back-shooter. The main thrust of the show examines the uses of any sort of morality as a cover for intolerance, and it is no accident that the men who beat the farmer so brutally wear hoods to cover their faces and that the hoods are recognized by the audience as similar to Ku Klux Klan uniforms. The idea of social responsibility is emphasized in the role of the schoolteacher and his attitude toward the actions of his pupils. Again there is a conscious attempt to call this role to the audience's attention as the farmer, storming into town for the final time, is stopped by the repentant teacher. He is brushed aside, however, and we are made to feel the folly of delaying the exercise of our social conscience. This role becomes even more crucial, of course, as the teacher brings the children to plead for the family to remain as members of the community. Finally, it is the children who express the central values of the episode. The children are the innocents, the hope of the future, misled only by the adult models of intolerance. The incredibly sentimentalized ending, with the presentation of the kitten as a token of understanding, brings the events to a tightly knit closing.

Such problems and such solutions might have occurred within the historical West, but they occur only rarely in the "Western," that creation of the popular mind which offers countless readers and viewers a way into and out of their fantasies, whatever they might be. The presentation of the problems and the attitudes expressed in this episode of "Gunsmoke" are specifically modern, contemporary attitudes. Not only are they alien to the classical Western, they are alien to the classical "Gunsmoke." Like so many other television series, so many formulas, "Gunsmoke" seems to have sought out its level of popularity. It remains in the prime-time lineup offering us such problems decked out in western finery. The Western formula with its honored code allows the problems to be defined in extreme and often violent terms that might seem unacceptable in other settings. The choices of the poor farmer are severely limited, as are the responses of his fellow townsmen. They are limited by the Western frame, which says that individuals do not have the variety of response that we know in our own experience. The use of violence in this world is permissible. The schoolteacher, free from the bureaucratic pressures of contemporary society and its complex educational system, is free to make his own mistakes and his own corrections. And the West, as the environment of optimism, lends itself to the positive outcome of the problem.

Clearly, what has happened is that television has made the Western into a lens through which we can view our contemporary culture. The lens is composed of all the elements of past forms and formulas, of history and legend, books, movies, radio serials. More importantly, it is composed of our knowledge of these things, our familiarity with the reality and with the artistic creations that rise from the reality. But there are other elements, too. The television Western must conform to the series format, with all the demands of repetition and all the prohibitions against any sort of ultimate change or development. Not only is it impossible for our heroes to be killed, a given in any truly popular form, it is also impossible for the television heroes to have memories. If, on occasion, the inhabitants of Dodge City remember that a certain event took place on another episode, that fact is scarcely able to alter the way in which they feel now. "Bonanza," then, early in its history can open a new season having dropped one of the four central characters. Brother Adam simply ceased to exist in the fictional world and, consequently, in the minds of the viewers. Only later, after years and years of *audience* definition, when the memory has been created in the mind of the *audience,* will the death of one of the characters force the show off the air.

In this circular framework the classic issues of western adventure would have played themselves out long ago. In order to avoid this the producers have applied the western vision to a host of other problems. The problem-solution paradigm of the sitcom and the family focus of the domestic comedy have been combined with the Western formula in the creation of a new form of popular art. It should come as no surprise that the mystery has developed in a similar manner.

4

MYSTERIES: ORDER AND AUTHORITY

Despite the lack of historical distance, the world of the mystery is as removed from the experience of most televiewers as that of the Western. At the same time, because of its contemporaneity, it is like another side of our own world, one that we know exists but that we may never see, may experience only in rare moments of extremity. Much of the appeal of the mystery story has always been this familiarity, the glimpse of something recognized but alien, tangible but inaccessible. Our interest is whetted by our knowledge that real criminals do exist, and we compare fictional crime with that reported in our newspapers and news broadcasts, hoping, perhaps, to find something that is as exciting as what we view as "entertainment." But it is hardly ever there.

So we turn to the world of the popular mystery story, expressed for us over and over again as novel, movie, radio series, comic strip, comic book. Here, as in the Western, are the events, patterns, and people with which we are immediately familiar. It is a world that carries its own limits, its own set of probabilities, its characters and character types, all of which build a separate reality within which the viewer/reader is an active participant. The inevitable movement from crime to capture, the pattern of events, clues, false leads, the brilliant deductions, all go to make up the puzzle, the game that intrigues millions of Americans. It is not so much a game of competition in which the audience attempts to discover the criminal before the detective does, as it is a game of titillation in which the audience is taken behind the scenes for a bit of excitement. Here the viewer is on safe grounds, given entry to a world of broken morals, broken bodies, broken people, and allowed to work through to the knowledge that some sort of correction has been affected and a rather satisfying conclusion has been reached. It is a safe world but exciting. It is predictable but varied. For television, then, the task is to draw on a vast body of material which could appeal to an already existing mass audience in an even more massive way, to use the mystery forms in existence, and to begin to adapt the form in terms of its own aesthetic attitudes, its own set of cultural expressions.

At the center of the mystery lies the crime. It is the event that precipitates all other events in the formula. It necessitates the existence of the detective or policeman and that ultimately defines much of the world in which it occurs. Most often in the popular mystery, the crime is murder, and as has often been pointed out, this event and its consequent unraveling are strongly molded in the Oedipal pattern. It is not crime as universal symbolic construct that is of interest here, however, so much as it is crime as cultural metaphor. What does crime mean in contemporary American popular entertainment? As such, the implications of the metaphor may vary, and the range of mystery story types is a result of the variation. On one level, crime, even murder, is merely the interruption of a well-ordered universe. In the mild English thriller and its American imitations, the murder must be solved by the essentially rational and intellectual detective, and the world will be once more set at rights. This is not to say that such crimes or such stories are to be taken lightly. As the recent play/movie *Sleuth* makes quite clear, such an attitude has at its base much more serious implications about the nature of humanity, of culture, and of the specific society in which such entertainments flourish. Those serious implications lie much closer to the surface in what has been described as the hard-boiled detective story, and it is this more American form that is the most recent antecedent for most of television's versions of the mystery.

In this harsher world the crime of murder is always expected, almost invited. It is a world limited to the fringes of society, to the slums and their inhabitants on the one hand and to high society on the other. It is not unusual to move in the course of a few pages or a few scenes from a series of sleazy bars, from conversations with small-time hoodlums and prostitutes, to the mansion overlooking Los Angeles or to the Manhattan penthouse. Everyone here is infected with the crimes that stand at the center of the action. The discovery of the murderer often leads us into the discovery of other crime, other murders, some committed by the same individuals, others committed long ago, or recently as acts of desperation. It is a world of half light, of half truth. There is no such thing as pure goodness, and by implication there is no such thing as total evil. People are motivated by greed, by lust, by jealousy, by moments of passion, and their actions involve them in strange webs of deceit and guilt.

Into such situations comes the detective, the central character on whom the actions of the story depend. He represents authority, which, to some degree, comes from the fact that he must be licensed by some formal agency. On rare occasions he is a policeman.

In any case, however, he participates much more fully in the partially defined world of crime than any official representative of the law. This is due in part to his knowledge of and willingness to use the techniques of those he seeks. Like the gunfighter, he is a violent man. He may also be gentle, moved by much of what he sees. Frequently he has great difficulty in establishing lasting human relationships, and his sexual life as depicted as part of the action of the novel or movie may be casual or intense, but never a source of final fulfillment. Some detectives are rather well educated, and references to literature or to art serve to point up their complex nature. Many of them are ex-policemen who have become finally convinced that the restrictions imposed by layers of officialdom serve to increase the possibilities for violent crime rather than to limit it. As a result, the detective is likely to be excessively cynical about the law, about society, and about human nature.

In spite of all these actions and reactions the detective remains our guide. He takes us into the world of pain and corruption and brings us out again in the end. Would we enter such a world without such a guide? Would we enter knowing beforehand that there might not be the safe conclusion at the final moment of tension? Could we stand such a world of violent sounds, of fists on flesh, and of gunshots if we did not know that as a particular episode of a radio series ended, Sam Spade or Boston Blackie would put the proper punch to one of the thugs that has led him into the lair of the boss and that all would be neatly wrapped up by the time the police arrived on the scene? The prospect of the mystery is one of forbidden excitement, and the detective allows us to experience it without being dirtied by it.

Such a guide is even more necessary, of course,
when the complexities are heightened and we begin
to admit not only the "badness" of the detective but
the "goodness" of the criminal as well. In seeing the
criminal as the rebel, the character who refuses to
be bound by social convention, as the character who
practices an American ethic of rugged individualism
at its purest, the criminal becomes, in Robert War-
show's words, the tragic hero. He is tragic obviously
because he must fail, but he is our hero in that he expresses all our own rebellious impulses. Such a conception is more pronounced in the history of the cinematic tradition than in the literary. Characters from
Little Caesar, through Scarface and Bonnie and
Clyde, to the Godfather loom on the heroic side in
their attempts to create alternative systems of crime
that are as powerful as the accepted system of legal-
ity in American culture and society. In the end the
mystery story, like all works of popular art, must sub-
stantiate the prevailing values of the audience. Those
values, no matter how significant the flirtation with
rebellion, will fall ultimately on the side of order and
justice and will be defined by the majority opinions of
what *should* be right. When the character of the criminal moves to the forefront, then, it is possible to say
that we have moved out of the realm of the mystery
story and into the art of character and cultural biography.

In the traditional mystery story, the popular formulas, the detective must remain as the central character *and* as the moral center of the work. His ambiguous character and social position serve as our key
to the moral judgments of the book. In the case of a
character such as Spillane's Mike Hammer, who ap-
propriates to himself the position of judge, jury, and

executioner, the ambiguity remains outside the book, with the audience. Whether or not one accepts Hammer's moral point of view is a point to be decided. Perhaps it is a key to Hammer's popularity that he behaves very much like the criminals whom he destroys but that he is not forced into tragic death at the conclusion. Like the criminal, he is a rebel against conventional society. Unlike the criminal, he does not become a victim. In a more complex character such as Ross MacDonald's Lew Archer the moral ambiguity lies at the center of the character's perception of himself, his self-conscious exploration of his role in society and in the particular story. Exhibiting yet another style is Sam Spade, who operates on the basis of a code of morality that binds him as strictly as any gunfighter is bound by the code of the West.

In this way the American mystery story revolves around and is defined by the character of the detective. The character becomes the key to the varied meanings opened in this highly traditional formula, and the Thin Man will not represent the same concepts as the Fat Man. Travis McGee will differ from Nero Wolfe in significant ways. All of them will see us immersed in a world of crime, will somehow discover the centers of guilt, and will bring us back to our safe position outside the novel, the movie, or the radio episode.

In spite of this combined success of the detective and the reader/viewer, the movement in and out of the world of crime is not ultimately a total affirmation. Unlike the Western, from which one emerges with the sense of real historical accomplishment, the feeling that good has triumphed and civilization has come to the frontier, the mystery world insists that crime will continue. The solution of one crime by one tough detective is a very partial action, and no one knows this better than the detective himself. It is the source of his cynicism. He believes in the real possibility of a real and potent evil. The mystery, then, is a closed form. There is none of the possibility of transcendence that we find in the Western. To some extent, of course, this is due to the fact pointed out earlier, that the world of the mystery is in most cases coexistent with our own. It is a very contemporary form, and each generation must create its own versions. The mythical or popular West, by definition, is the land of hope and possibility. The mythical world of the mystery story is a dark place in which men of very limited power clear up individual difficulties. There is no sense that the solution of one of these murders, even when a nest of murders is solved in the process, will enable society to proceed in a better, purer way. What the creation of the American version of the mystery story suggests is that our own world is filled with violence and evil. More than that, it tells us that the clearing away of violence and evil, despite our historical successes. is not a simple matter.

Of course, all of this analysis is directed toward the forms that flourished prior to the television versions of the mystery. In an even narrower sense it is directed only to the hard-boiled American portion of those antecedent forms. There are thousands of polite, puzzle-type mystery stories in which the sense of evil as reality is minimized by the rationality and intellect of the detective, the lighthearted humor of husband-wife detective teams, or the overwhelming force of authority. But the producers of television entertainment learned early that many of the elements of popular mysteries are the bread-and-butter elements of their own shows. Violence, action, adventure, tension, and excitement are necessary, or so it seems, to maintain a whetted appetite in the massive TV audiences. It should also be pointed out here that the mystery has at its heart that old idea of solving a problem. It would be stretching a point to say that the vicious world of a show such as "Hawaii Five-O" is merely a tense version of "I Love Lucy," but both the attitude taken on the mystery and the slapstick violence of the Lucy show indicate that the relationship is a complex one. The task for the mystery show producer is to walk the thin line between what is permissible in the way of violence and what is permissible in the way of moral judgment. Cynicism, the failure of authority, the corruption of society, the rewards of crime: how are these to be presented to a mass audience through a medium that is delicately sensitive to public opinion, official as well as private? The choices for program material reflect the various means by which producers and program directors can mediate somehow between mass entertainment and social respectability.

From the beginning there was a vast body of material waiting for television adaptation. Some of the more famous literary detectives had already made one media leap to become the central characters of radio series. To be sure, this had required a degree of "toning down." It was not possible to broadcast some of the things that one was permitted to read about. Such situations became even more restricted when the audience could actually see what these characters were doing, and the visual aspect made for greater problems in the face of a growing relationship among sponsors, the public, and the content of the show. In response to multiple pressures, one answer is to produce a series in which many difficulties are eliminated from the beginning by the premises on which the show is created. Such a show can cater to all the desires of the most public of art forms. It can satisfy official restrictions, maintain the prevailing public ethic, and at the same time, thrill and entertain its audiences with action and excitement. The more "realistic" the show, the better. So we come to "Dragnet."

This show is not about detectives in the classic, hard-boiled sense, nor about the beautiful and strange women who come knocking at detectives' doors, nor about crime as metaphor or murder as Oedipal complex. From the opening sequence of narrator's voice over aerial shots of Los Angeles to the concluding report on the fate of the offenders, "Dragnet" creates a documentary tone that argues for itself the portrayal of truth rather than fiction. As the camera moves slowly over an expanse of urban sprawl, the narrator tells us that this is the city. We cannot deny our eyes, so his credibility is assured. Somehow it does not seem so absurd for him to tell us what is obvious; rather, in the face of other TV shows, it is reassuring to receive such bald fact. The tone of his voice has a great deal to do with this establishment of fact, too, for it is a weary voice, somewhat hard, but without the flippance that would characterize a private detective. The voice offers us some statistics—on population, on the number of crimes committed here each day, each hour. The details might change from week to week, but the pattern remains the same and reaches the final point in the introduction as we are told that the narrator works in the city, that his name is Joe Friday, that he is a cop. A policeman; he is a cop. Then the famous musical theme, the four chords, pounded at us by a full orchestra.

The music will carry us through the episode, punctuating moments of high drama, underlining the ironies created by these policemen as if the ironies were not sufficiently blatant in themselves. The music transposes from dialogue to narration to action. We always come back to Friday's voice giving us the date of the events, the time of each segment of the narrative, information on the weather, the attitudes of his colleagues. This factual list of times and dates, the use of place names and street identification, serve to maintain the documentary aspect of the show. As audience we know that the events are "true," that they have been adapted from the files of the Los Angeles Police Department, and that only the names have been changed to protect the innocent. We assume that the dates and the time sequences, then, must correspond to that case history, to the solution of the crime as it "actually happened."

The documentary format is carried over into the style of the actors. Joe Friday is portrayed by Jack Webb, the show's producer, and is as lean and hard as his voice. His close-cropped hair and sad eyes speak of a weariness with his ugly world. He and his partners represent the epitome of the professional police detective. Everything is low-key. The tone, even of humorous situations, is quiet, and it takes only a bitter grin, a sort of sagging chuckle, to show us that even the lighter moments are filled with bitterness. A standard element of the "Dragnet" formula is the squelching of any attempt on the part of an involved party to interject personality, a skewed or personal version of the meaning of an event or series of events. The meaning of the show is summed up in such situations when Friday and his partner exchange rueful glances and insist that they be told the facts, "Just the facts, ma'am."

The implications of the show are clear. A fact is different from a fiction, from a story. A fact can be evaluated on the basis of external norms. One set of facts can be judged to be in conflict with another. When this happens, the perpetrators of the "incorrect" set may be sought and punished by the defenders of the other set. No room for ambiguity here, and no room for individual style, the hallmark of the pop detective. There is no way for a detective to take the law into his own hands, to destroy evil because it exists and constitutes a personal affront. Evil does exist, but as an affront to society. There are no private codes by which an individual may avenge the death of his friend. The only code is that of the city of Los Angeles, county of Los Angeles, state of California. The ultimate meaning of the show is that the authority legally constituted with the police is the proper authority to be used in the detection of criminal action. It is also true that we return week after week because the police detective, like his flashier private counterpart, is no Western hero capable of cleaning up the town in one swoop of action. As in the hard-boiled story, evil remains, is a part of the society. We assume that the files of the LAPD are endless and that script after script will flow into "Dragnet." From Joe Friday's point of view that simply means that he has a job to do, that he can report to work each morning as expected to begin investigation of his current assignment. Crime is not a moral fable. It is a counterproductive force that must be reckoned with in social terms. Those are the facts. The result, the reckoning that does take place, is exhibited for us with the "true" ending, the narrator's reading of the criminal's sentence. Then, once again as in the opening of the show, we see the huge badge filling the entire screen.

It is an impressive style and one that was widely copied. Doubtless many individuals formed their ideas about the interior of police stations by watching "The Lineup." Many youngsters playing cops and robbers learned their proper radio jargon by watching Broderick Crawford barking "Ten Four" into a microphone on "Highway Patrol." These shows and others like them used the factual background of police files for their sources. Others imitated the documentary style and implied that they, too, based their material on "fact." "M Squad" and "Naked City" achieved, at various times, the same sort of "realism" and became highly popular series. The type continues with the federal version in "The FBI," which not only uses actual case histories as "source materials" but has the thanks of the director of the FBI and his associates publicly announced in the closing titles of each episode. Such shows continue to reflect a major television attitude toward crime.

This is not to say, however, that the primary type of television mystery entertainment has this factual base as its major artistic device. Throughout the period of "Dragnet's" greatest popularity other shows were being developed that offered other versions of the meaning of crime and justice. In these forms as in the earlier literary and cinematic types, the character of the detective becomes the primary mode of determining the attitude toward what goes on within the formulas. One of the most popular and important shows in the development of the TV mystery is the "Perry Mason" series, begun in 1957, five years after "Dragnet." Mason, of course, came from the novels of Erle Stanley Gardner and was a prime choice to fill a

weekly slot of television time. The series seemed to
mediate between the more hard-boiled detectives and
the factual police-oriented shows by offering a complex who-done-it framework for murder.

Working primarily outside and frequently in apparent competition with the police, Mason reflects in
a complex way the prevailing cultural attitude and
thrills his audiences while finally reaffirming their
values. Much of his ability to do this rises from Mason's
position in the society. He is not a detective, but a
lawyer, and as such he stands in the long tradition of
the enlightened amateur. There have always been
the solvers of crime who are not detectives, but who
are merely the country parson or the local doctor. To
Perry Mason people bring what are essentially legal
problems, and in the course of the defense of his
clients he is forced to unravel the solutions to the murders for which they are wrongly accused. The series
of actions by which Mason becomes involved is highly
formulaic, and almost every episode develops in a similar manner.

Before the titles of the show are flashed on the
screen we see individuals in conflict. They may be
arguing, involved in physical struggle, exchanging
angry words over the telephone. A car may be seen
speeding out of a driveway, or a conversation may
be overheard by servants. In the second stage of this
conflict the audience is made aware that a murder has
been committed. We see a victim pleading for his or
her life before shots are fired. There is the discovery
of a body. Perhaps the police arrive, summoned mys-
teriously to the scene of the crime. In no case, however, is the audience permitted to see the actual murderer.

Now Mason is introduced to the case. At times, he,

too, has been notified of the crime by a mysterious source. In other arrangements we may move directly to his office and discover some concerned person pleading with him to accept the case and defend the jailed suspect. In this way we are also introduced to Mason's team of associates. Paul Drake, the private investigator, represents the more physical aspects of the case. He will probe private lives, follow up leads, trace missing persons. Della Street, the ever-present secretary, represents the mental activity that will be involved, and is always armed with a stenographic pad in which she records essential details.

Once Mason agrees to defend the suspect, the audience is sure of the person's innocence. Then begins the elaborate game that moves toward the establishment of that innocence. In the first phase there must be the discovery of essential clues, the establishment of a time sequence, the opening developments that will lead to a highly complex series of personal relationships involving not only the official suspect but a host of individuals surrounding the suspect and/or victim. Out of this group must come the real murderer.

In the first courtroom sequence Mason will be on the defensive as the district attorney methodically begins to build a case. Evidence is presented that clearly links the suspect to the act of murder. The motive is established. Meanwhile, Drake continues his search for clues, and Della records the bits and pieces of evidence so that Mason's own picture of the crime begins to develop.

In the scene of disclosure Mason is on the offensive, even though the DA may not have concluded his own case. Frequently Perry recalls a witness whom he had barely questioned earlier. More commonly this scene is used for the portrayal of his famous courtroom showmanship. He is likely to ask permission to bring things into the courtroom, blackboards or charts, bales of hay into which the murder weapon might be fired. At times he asks the entire court to move out of the courtroom, to some unrelated location or to the scene of the crime. The audience knows now that Perry has firmly established the innocence of his client and has most probably determined the identity of the guilty party. The camera contributes to our suspense at this point as it roams the courtroom focusing on the tense faces of possible suspects, enticing us to reproduce the line of Mason's thought so that we, too, may catch the criminal.

Relentless pressure begins to build until finally someone must break as true guilt and the real web of motivation are established. An involved party cracks, points a guilty finger, and the murderer leaps to his or her feet in a futile attempt to flee the courtroom. The murderer is placed on the stand and there breaks into sobs of penitence or cries of anger, arguing that the victim deserved to die. Even when he and the audience tend to agree, Mason must always put the rhetorical question and ask whether or not an innocent party should be convicted for the victim's death.

Throughout this process of discovery and defense Mason has been depicted not only as intelligent, rational, and compassionate but as a shrewd and intuitive thinker. It is his ability to perceive what is hidden, his ability to discover undisclosed human relationships, that enables him to defend his client most effectively. For those hidden relationships always seem to indicate hidden motives for illegal actions, violent and murderous. To Mason it is obvious that facts, events, clues, and these human entanglements may have multiple meanings and implications. It is the discovery of these meanings and implications that enables him to appear almost as a wizard, a man of magic, in the solving of crimes, in the discovery of solutions to problems, and in overcoming the threat of unjust punishment which hangs over the head of his client.

His magic is heightened by the fact that there are others involved in this action who are looking at the same facts, the same events, the same human beings, and are somehow reaching different conclusions which will end in punishing a client for actions not committed. These people are portrayed as the representatives of social authority. Lieutenant Tragg as the police investigator is always pitted against Paul Drake. Tragg is old, short, dumpy, gruff, hardheaded to the point of stubbornness. Drake is young, smooth, suave, well dressed, with a bright smile and a sense of humor. He is always able to discover what Tragg, with all his dedication and goodwill, has overlooked. Mason's opponent is District Attorney Hamilton Burger, who is given to exasperation. He cannot follow Mason's trains of thought. He frequently interrupts and objects to the more flamboyant activities of his opponent. He is continually calling on the judge to rule Mason's antics out of order. Always, he fails to see the relevance of a certain argument until it is too late for him to counter. Mason, on the other hand, is capable of intuitive leaps, of seeing what is hidden and pointing it out as if it were obvious. Tragg and his associates, Burger and his assistants, are always made out to be the dupes at the end of the situation. They remain on good terms with Mason—the groups are sometimes seen together at the close of the trial—but we are never allowed to forget that the police and the authorities have misread the facts which to Perry Mason obviously pointed to the innocence of his client. Similarly, we are never allowed to overlook the fact that Mason finds the true criminal, establishes real guilt, while he frees his client.

The implication is that facts and appearances are not always indicative of the "truth." If Joe Friday insists on "just the facts," and if he presents them to someone like Hamilton Burger, it is quite likely that innocent people must suffer the consequences unless a Perry Mason intervenes. He knows that guilt, to some degree, is universal, that even the most innocent of persons may have something to hide, some past action, some entanglement, which under certain circumstances may serve as the motivation for an action as violent as murder. Perhaps even the audience cannot escape such guilt. This world is much more akin to that of the private detective of literature and of the movies and radio. The argument of the show is, of course, that Mason serves a higher authority than that represented by Tragg and Burger. He serves the truth, which is always indicated in the titles by the statue of justice.

As a representative of the legal profession Mason is dedicated to something more than a judicial code. One cannot help but question the effectiveness of that code when week after week Mason cuts into the power and intellect of his opponents. We are titillated by the fact that he drives to the scene of the crime in a long, sleek, black Cadillac convertible just as Tragg emerges on the scene in his own puffing fashion in a squad car. Mason is like the opposite and polite side of Mike Hammer. While Spillane's character subverts authority by utilizing vigilante tactics, Mason challenges the same authority with an appeal to its ultimately finer qualities.

The camera fades away from the team of happy associates, and the audience is likely to join in this finale, for Mason's appeal rises from his verve, his flash, his wit, and he joins the rank of the traditional private detective who somehow seems to transcend the limits imposed on those of us who submit to more normal restrictions and who lead, as a result, more mundane lives.

Though the police documentary and the private-eye traditions stand as major developments in the television mystery, a third type currently dominates. The type is important because it links the mystery—that brutal and unfamiliar world—with the world that is closer to us. As with the Western the link does not always come from content. Rather, the structure of the new mysteries is crucial to our developing conception of a television formula.

The new type is a hybrid. It combines the appeal of the rebellious, anti-authority figure with the official, mainstream, authoritative morality of the police documentary. As such it satisfies the audience need for excitement and glamour, with the always present assurance that official representatives are not the dupes that the private eye would seem to indicate. Attached to official agencies, these characters are free of the drudgery experienced by a Joe Friday. The worlds they move in, the adventures they survive, are as unrealistic as those of the most eccentric private investigator. This flair for adventure is obviously one of the greatest sources of their appeal. As in the classic private-detective tradition, the real key to understanding the differences among these figures is in the individual style, and the conceptions of justice are embodied in the strange combinations that occur. What television now offers in the area of mystery entertainment is a world of personality. Each star brings a different view of the process of solution, a different attitude toward the nature of crime. The struggle is not between good and evil, for as in all popular formulas we know that there is no real contest there. Rather, the struggle is between a certain type of detective and the very idea of crime.

In "McMillan and Wife" McMillan solves a crime in each episode, usually with the direct aid of his wife. He is supposed to be the commissioner of police in San Francisco. Yet instead of glimpses into the life of a harried administrator, we get the adventures of a totally autonomous detective. One of the chief defining characteristics of the series is the humor, and McMillan's wife, detective assistant, and house maid are all comic characters. One of the most recurring themes has to do with the commissioner's private life, and he is constantly interrupted in amorous moments with his wife by calls that drag him from bed. It is not at all unusual to see him involved in a hilarious chase along the cable car tracks or diving into the bay in an attempt to rescue his wife who is floating out to sea in an empty beer barrel. It is all like a great game.

"McCloud" is a deputy marshal from Taos, New Mexico, who has been assigned to the New York City Police Department. Here the contrast between the values of McCloud, transplanted Western hero, and the hard-nosed, book-abiding New York cops gives us our cue. He manages to carry his revolver, wear his boots and Stetson, and in the titles of each episode ride a horse down one of New York's busier avenues. For him crime is a great deal simpler than the rule books indicate, and the conflict between McCloud and the police captain is as prevalent as the conflict between law and criminality. For the audience he expresses a clearer, simpler set of anticrime values in which there is little need to read the criminal his rights before making an arrest. Such a view might become highly cynical if adopted by the New York police themselves. Coming from the cowboy it is permissible.

For "Columbo," too, the test is like a game, but of a more sinister sort. Columbo pursues each criminal —whom the audience knows from the opening moments of each episode—with a combination of comic bumbling, sloppiness, and good nature. In addition to the identity of the criminal, however, the audience knows that beneath this façade Columbo is a super-sleuth. In the final moments when the criminal has trapped himself because he has been finagled into revealing his true character while misreading Columbo's ability, the audience is reassured that the slickness and planning of the criminal are not worth the effort. Columbo is like a vital and nagging conscience. His surface appearance is as nothing compared to the moral patchwork constructed by the villain.

While there are numerous characters who develop their personalities into the themes of series, another group of shows takes this same pattern and redefines the whole popular genre from which it emerges. These shows also depend on a central character who is attached in a semiofficial manner to an official agency, but around that central character is developed a strong family-type structure. The star looms as the father type, whose authority, by virtue of the world of the mystery, takes on societal as well as domestic proportions. The families that are developed here, like the "family" of "Gunsmoke," are not biologically related. They are groups of closely knit individuals who function as interdependent units both emotionally and intellectually. There is every indication that the ties that bind them are as strong as or stronger than blood ties, and in any given episode the crucial point of the plot may have to do with the family situation. In such dramas crime becomes more than the social threat. It becomes the device through which the audience explores interpersonal relationships. These relationships become the foundation on which social relationships are created, so that while the crime is always solved, our attention is usually focused on the way in which the personal matters must be clarified prior to the solution of the criminal problem. This is not to say that the producers have fallen back on the old "environment as stimulus" argument as the cause of crime, though that might occur in an individual episode. The more important observation is that social and environmental situations actually reflect more basic human patterns. The individual human beings remain the focus even in the most scathing indictments of social forces.

"The Rookies," for example, focuses on a small group of special police officers recruited from what would be considered nontraditional types for police careers. They have entered police work because of strong moral impulses toward helping people, helping society. They come from college or from experiences in Vietnam, and they frequently find their own considerations to be at odds with those of the tough old police sergeant who is responsible for their training and for their actions. He becomes the father figure when we realize that he isn't so tough beneath his stony exterior. In a recent episode two of the rookies, one black, one white, take on an assignment in a tough ghetto neighborhood where they hope to establish rapport with a gang of delinquents. The white man has very idealistic notions about what is possible. The black man, who grew up in the neighborhood, is constantly warning his friend away from do-good impulses. In the midst of a gang war, which the two policemen allow to take place in hopes of shaming the participants, one of the gang leaders is shot. The rookies are thoroughly reprimanded for their foolish application of such a softheaded approach. They return to the gang as policemen and remind the young men over and over that they are cops, not social workers. As cops they solve the mystery of the shooting; the gang leader's greatest admirer had accidentally shot his hero while trying to be "tough." Everyone learns from the experience. The gang leader sees that his demands for toughness had ruined his young admirer, that his position of leadership makes demands on him as a model for younger members of the neighborhood. The white policeman learns that goodwill is not enough. The black policeman learns that his neighborhood can be redeemed. The sergeant learns that his men are capable of difficult tasks and that at times their own instincts must be trusted. It is a lesson that many fathers must learn as their children grow up. All the policemen, despite disclaimers to being social workers, have displayed social worker concerns in solving a variety of personal problems. They have applied few traditional law enforcement methods in the process. Such a show, obviously, is far removed from "Dragnet."

"Mod Squad" follows a similar pattern, though here the young officers work as undercover agents as the police department's answer to the counter culture. A young white woman, a white man, and a black man constitute the team, which is supervised by a police captain, increasingly parental in his concern. Even more than in the other series, the action of "Mod Squad" focuses on the failures of human relationships. Each member of the team comes from a background deprived in some way of normal homelife. The argument is that they are more sensitive because of this, and the solution to crimes and the punishment of guilty individuals are almost always tempered by their concern for broken human beings. Frequently the individuals of the team serve as the focus for an episode, and the concern of the other members becomes the central device on which action is built.

This is also the case with "Ironside," one of the most professional and impressive of the family syndrome series. Ironside is a former chief of police in San Francisco who has been paralyzed from the waist down by a sniper's bullet. He browbeats his commissioner into making him the leader of a special investigation team. It is the team that becomes the family. The young white police officer, the young white female police officer, and the young black assistant are more like brothers and sister than professional associates, and Ironside himself is the gruff, businesslike, all-caring father. As with the "Gunsmoke" group we have seen real developments among these people. Mark, the young black, began by pushing Ironside's wheelchair and driving his van. Cured of bitterness and racism by Ironside's trust, he has now finished college and law school and is becoming a police officer. Only a few years ago the profession stood for him as a symbol of oppression. During this time the white assistants have progressed from naïve trainees into cold-nerved professionals. The relationships among the group have become less professional and more loving with each season's series, and the content of the episodes has shifted from adventurous crime-chase-capture to social concern of a vitally human sort. Moral responsibility of individuals, official as well as private, often becomes the topic in question in such shows, as is illustrated by the following examples.

Ed Brown, the white police assistant, loses his identification and is arrested after being mugged. As the officers deal with him roughly, ignoring his rights as a citizen, he decides to see how far they will go and refuses to offer help in identifying himself. As a result, he is booked, jailed, and spends several days and nights in the lockup. No one makes an attempt to think of him as a human being, and he is plagued with flashback memories of his own actions with regard to criminals who might have been as innocent as he is now. The worried Ironside finally locates him in jail, but intuitively decides not to acknowledge him. Ed, too, refuses to recognize his mentor. Ed is learning in a painful but rewarding way, and like all good fathers, Ironside knows that such learning is the best kind. In an explicit reference to Christ's agony, Ironside says that the experience is Ed's Calvary. Finally, unable to stand the strain of being treated as an animal, Ed screams to be released. The local authorities follow up on his case, learn that he is indeed a police officer, and release him. While doing so they reprimand him and remind him that police authorities are supposed to stick together, not to criticize one another. But we know that Ed Brown will be a different sort of policeman after this experience, and the social criticism is clear for the home audience. If law and order are not tempered with mercy and justice, as they must be in a family, there is no hope for an ordered society.

Another episode shifts the same sort of responsibility to the ordinary citizen and to the viewing audience. A young woman has been murdered in plain view and in hearing range of a densely populated area. No one has come to her aid. Ironside arranges a television special devoted to the problem of individual civic responsibility. A panel of experts from government, religion, and psychology discuss the moral aspects of the problem while Ironside appears repeatedly to call for help from any individual who might have information regarding the murder. We are constantly reminded of the human aspect of the problem by large, full-screen photographs of the young victim and by comments from her friends and family. Unknown to the producers or participants in the show, Ironside has already located his suspect and is using the show as a means of forcing the killer to identify himself. The fictional audience of Ironside's fictional program and we, the actual audience of this episode, are given ample opportunity to consider the social aspects of the crime while we are able to watch the fear, the agony, and the final disintegration of the murderer. It is like a play within a play, with our own, real world as the larger frame. We see the murderer's wife reach the inevitable conclusion that her husband is guilty, that she should not have lied about his whereabouts on the night of the murder in a futile attempt to save her marriage. We see the murderer in a hopeless attempt to save himself, drawn to the television studio, trying to pass himself off as a concerned citizen who has information to offer. The entire program forces all involved groups to reconsider the nature of their responsibility to other human individuals, again, to the ways in which we constitute a social family.

This trend in television mysteries reached its furthest extension in a short-lived series called "Sarge."

Sarge was cop turned priest. In the pilot episode we saw the bombing of his young wife. After apprehending the killers who had acted out of revenge and were attempting to kill Sarge rather than his wife, he decides not to return to his position as a police detective. Instead, he pursues a calling given up years before. He overcomes immense prejudice and his own lack of training, completes the necessary seminary work, and becomes the spiritual leader of an urban parish. But he cannot escape crime; the implied question, of course, is Who can? His activities are divided between counseling and short-cutting the efforts of the police. He is the father figure made all too explicit; his combination of detective expertise and ultimate, metaphysical family approach somehow strain credulity to the breaking point.

Recent shows, more realistic in tone, have turned again to the hard-hitting police professional. But shows such as "Police Story," though they do not focus on a continuing set of characters that become family-directed in their relationships, do suggest that the "fraternity" of policemen functions in a personal manner. Similarly, our attention is now directed to the fact that the professional also has another life, that there are real families behind men who serve as social protectors. Much of the action of such shows involves the interpersonal relationships of the central figures.

Television has made of the mystery formula, as with the Western, something more than it has traditionally been. In the changing formulaic patterns that occur within this single form we can see the movement toward an overriding television attitude that minimizes traditional distinctions among the popular arts and unites them in a single pattern of values. They are

values expressive of a dreamlike age in which sup-
posedly simpler issues could be solved by direct action
and by reliance on close personal relationships. It is
as if the world of the situation and domestic comedy had been shifted out of doors and into the streets.
Moving from the immediate internal problems of
the family to the external issues involving the "social
family," the harsher forms have moved inward again
with their concentration on close groups and interpersonal relationships.

Authority, expressed in the wise father figure, is the
chief implement for change in this world. It serves to
preserve order where the chaos of criminality threat-
ens to touch individuals and the society they constitute. It offers a sense of continuity and wisdom in the
midst of rapid change and unsteady beliefs.

The issues examined are removed from our worlds
of experience by virtue of their inclusion in the Western and the mystery. Similarly, the heroic figures
who can solve the problems of these worlds are remote, despite their fatherly characterization. Television does turn to problems related directly to those
of the audience, and to figures who populate a more
realistic world, in the formulas of the doctor and lawyer shows. In these shows the values approached
obliquely in the more violent forms become the central subject matter.

5

DOCTORS AND LAWYERS:
COUNSELORS AND CONFESSORS

"Owen Marshall, Counselor-at-Law" is the most recent of a long and noble line of television lawyers. In the past we have seen the lawyer as detective with "Perry Mason," the lawyer as protector of constitutional rights with "The Defenders," the lawyer as glamour figure with "Judd for the Defense," and the lawyer as public protector with "The Young Lawyers" and "The Storefront Lawyers." Marshall's most recent ancestor, however, is none of these. Owen Marshall is son of "Marcus Welby, M.D.," which comes from a distinguished line of its own. The names ring loud in the history and legend of television: "Medic," "Ben Casey," "Dr. Kildare," and the cryptic, yet somehow forceful, "The Doctors" and "The Nurses." The continuing popularity of the two formulas is evidenced by the number of shows that might be compared with Welby and Marshall. "The Bold Ones" provides an umbrella for both types, alternating a team of lawyers with a team of doctors. "Medical Center," reminiscent in some ways of older medical shows, provides competition for Welby. All of these shows, presented in prime time, are preceded during the day by a host of soap opera doctors and lawyers, whose actions as professionals lead directly to the more dramatic aspects of their private lives. Such relationships, of course, historical and contemporary, are obvious. What is perhaps not so obvious is the membership of Welby and Marshall in a larger family. Both shows are clearly dependent on the formulaic elements that we have established in other more unrelated types such as the sitcom, the domestic comedy, and the new Westerns and mysteries.

It should come as no surprise, then, that Robert Young, star-father of "Father Knows Best," should be chosen to play the title role of Marcus Welby. Aged but no less wise, he heals his patients with a mixture of medical expertise and fatherly compassion. In a more complex manner the fictional frame is broken and we see Young as "himself" advising senior citizens of their Medicare benefits in an announcement produced by the Department of Health, Education, and Welfare. Arthur Hill, star of "Owen Marshall," performs a similar function when he introduces a television audience to four nights of the Russian film version of Tolstoy's *War and Peace*. Where are the "real" doctors who could advise people of their health benefits? Would Young be suitable for such a role if he were not seen each week as Welby? Would Hill be chosen to lead us into the complexities of Tolstoy if he were not adept at explaining for his weekly audience the intricacies of legal and moral responsibility? He points out that we, like many of Tolstoy's characters, live in tumultuous times in which the ground seems to shift beneath our feet and in which we frequently turn to our leaders for guidance. And he points out Tolstoy's clear indication that the ground is not always so stable under the feet of the leaders. Do we accept his statements, his analysis of the state of our world? To whom do we turn if we cannot shift painful responsibility onto the shoulders of those who seek it, our television counselors?

Again, such observations about the uses and similarities of these "characters" should not be surprising. They touch only the surface of television's complexity. Medical and legal shows expand what have become basic television elements into what would appear to be a wider world than that of the sitcom, the domestic comedy, or the Western and the mystery. In some ways that is indeed the case. In other ways we find ourselves returning again to a recurring pattern: failure, response, and solution.

From one point of view such a world would seem to be far removed from any sort of common experience in which "real" doctors and lawyers perform services that all of us need from time to time. Yet these television professionals are real enough as part of our experience. Welby and Marshall are real people for thousands of viewers. Patients become annoyed when their doctors do not behave as Welby does. Students at all levels discuss Marshall's cases. Families follow the exploits of their favorites. Even the nonviewer cannot escape the discussions that are carried on about him. When Robert Young is invited to give the commencement address at the University of Michigan Medical School, when a group protests with a counter commencement of its own, news is made. Marcus Welby appears on the evening news broadcast as well as on his own show. Because of this, the viewer is rewarded with more shows based on problems that might occur in his or her own experiences, with characters whose lives resemble his or her own in some particulars, with settings and situations rooted in "facts" which might also appear in the news.

In a recent episode of "Owen Marshall" the lawyer is called to the home of a friend who has just been raped. He arrives to discover two policemen "questioning" his client-friend in a calloused and suggestive manner, humiliating her with their lack of belief in her story. In spite of this the woman identifies her attacker as a fellow employee at a local hospital and files a complaint against him. When the wife of the accused man provides a strong alibi, the victim is forced to drop the case. The social attitude represented by the patrolmen in the opening scene is carried through as the woman loses her job and her standing in the community. In the course of these events she discovers several other women who have suffered similar attacks from the same young man, but who have not gone to the police for fear of public humiliation and harm to their families. Owen now suggests that his client bring a civil charge against the rapist, and she does so hoping to persuade the other women to testify.

During the trial the lawyers discover that all the attacked women are the wives of military officers serving in Vietnam, an observation that suggests a psychological pattern behind the attacks. An expert witness testifies to the effect that such aggression is often a form of transferred anger, an attempt to strike at an individual by hurting those near him. In more complex situations the disturbed individual may even strike at twice-removed figures, at individuals whose roles merely parallel those of the original object of transference. We learn that the defendant has been dishonorably discharged for failing to obey orders under fire. Hating the officer who caused him this humiliation, he transfers his anger to the wives of officers, attacking while the husbands are on active duty. Though it appears that the case is solved, the alibi of the defendant's wife remains as a firm obstacle. In order to break that alibi, Marshall's assistant arranges for the other victims to enter the courtroom during a moment of particular stress in the cross-examination of the defendant. Fearing that their presence indicates that they will testify, the defendant breaks down on the stand and confesses. His wife admits her perjury and requests psychiatric aid for her husband.

Such a story opens walls for the viewer, throws off the restrictions of the "living room" design we discovered in more closed forms. The issues are social problems, broad and familiar: rape, police attitudes, personal privacy, Vietnam, the returning veteran. Problems and questions: who is to blame, what has the war done to America, whose rights are to be respected, protected? Such issues frame the larger world of television. Like issues from the world of our own experience, they demand the explanations of experts and the guidance of those experienced in handling them.

The most important factor in that larger world is the star of the series. His function in the medical or legal show, and in all other dramatic series, is significantly different from the star function in the situation and domestic comedy. There, as evidenced by the names of the series, the audience is interested in viewing the performance of a "real" person. When one tunes in to "The Lucy Show," "The Mary Tyler Moore Show," "The New Dick Van Dyke Show," and similar forms, one tunes in to watch Lucille Ball, Mary Tyler Moore, or Dick Van Dyke. Distinctions between person and role are unclear—obviously Lucille Ball off camera behaves differently from the way she behaves before it. But Lucy's fictional character is less important to the audience than what Lucy is famous for. The fictional "role" assumed by the character is of secondary importance, as is evidenced by the fact that in the three shows just mentioned the fictional character retains the first name of the "real" person. Similarly, in domestic comedy, the audience is interested in observing the performances of Father, Mother, brother, sister. The focus is on the role and on the way the role is portrayed by favorites, rather than on the presentation of a totally fictitious character.

By contrast the dramatic series is characterized by the dual function of the star. As we have seen, there is something very appropriate about the fact that Robert Young plays Marcus Welby. And no doubt careful search was made in order to associate the proper "star" qualities of Arthur Hill with the character of Owen Marshall. Significantly, Hill has said that his portrayal of the character is modeled on his father, a "real life" attorney. In either case, however, it is Welby or Marshall rather than Young or Hill in whom the audience is primarily interested. And it is quite possible that it is Young as Welby rather than Young as Young who appeals to the audience of the HEW commercial for Medicare. The character moves into "life" rather than the "person" moving into the character as in sitcom.

This different kind of appeal rises in part from the fact that such characters are much more complex than the characters in the more simple formulas. Slapstick comedians and wise parents can be expected to behave in highly predictable, one-dimensional ways. Similarly, the shows in which they appear are structured around formulas that are highly repetitive and predictable. By contrast, Welby and Marshall exhibit a wide range of possibilities for character development. They are often angry with their patients and clients or with their associates. They interact with the other members of the cast, exhibiting a capacity for growth and learning. Their compassion and wisdom extend into all areas of society, to all age groups, and to all types of individuals. Part of their wisdom stems from the fact that they are able to respond to complex and ambiguous behavior, a behavior that more closely approaches our sense of reality than anything found in the more simple formulaic patterns. Ultimately, of course, these more complex formulas are still formulas: predictable, repetitive, essentially static. Marcus Welby can no more decide to leave the practice of medicine than Lucy can cease to get herself into impossible positions. If Welby did leave, he would no longer be Welby. The star system and the continuing series format leave much to be desired in the representation of reality. Nevertheless, the medical and legal shows create characters in whom we are interested as characters. In doing so they approach more traditional forms of art. More contemporary than the Western, less restricted than the mystery, more human than the situation and domestic comedy, these characters begin to populate a video world that coexists with our factual world.

Such characters did not spring overnight from the brain of a writer. Owen Marshall and Marcus Welby, as we have already seen, are evolutionary products, derived from other types of medical and legal shows and from other, more remote formulas. They are based on moments in cultural history which again reflect an older, more stable set of values. An examination of the evolutionary process within these two formulas will indicate distinctions among them, and point to the factors in the most recent formula that help to explain their popularity and cultural significance.

One of the great moments in television's version of

the medical profession has to be found in an episode of "Medic" that dealt with the problem of acne. The show centered on the problems of a young boy caught in the agonies of adolescence. In the course of the episode he learns that his drastic appearance can be treated medically, that he will not spend the next four or five years shielding his face behind his school books, lonely and frightened of girls. At one point the boy is addressed by the doctor, played by Richard Boone. The camera moves in for a close-up of Boone's face, and for all practical purposes he speaks directly to the audience. While he explains the causes and treatments of acne, we are forced to examine the marred and pocked terrain of his own face. He offers himself as an example of the fact that acne is serious, that it is not to be treated with the creams and devices advertised in comic books.

Boone as actor represents the professional. His assurance and skill are the focus of his shows. His understanding of human nature is essentially analytical and objective, and in most cases he defines a rather removed position from his patients. "Medic" depended on its realistic approach to define the role of the doctor in society, and Boone's face served more as a piece of evidence in a documentary than as a fictional mirror of compassion.

The next generation of medical shows, however, combined this professional approach with the personal, offering us sets of characters who could extend the range of plot possibilities and audience interests. The two most memorable series of this type are "Dr. Kildare" and "Ben Casey." Both shows center on the relationship of an older and younger doctor. As we follow Kildare through student and intern days to his completed M.D., we follow the growing relationship of the young man and his mentor, Dr. Gillespie. In "Ben Casey" the central character is a trained neurosurgeon who, nevertheless, must frequently defer to the judgment, age, and wisdom of Dr. Zorba. These shows are inwardly focused on the problems of the central characters. Events occurring in the hospitals give rise to problems that the doctors must face. In this way the formula resembles that of the domestic comedy, and both shows clearly depend on the father-son relationship that develops between the pairs of characters. In some cases the problems are of a general nature, involving the emotional coming of age of the younger men. In most instances, however, the conflict is structured around a more specialized situation; we watch what might be called the professional coming of age of young doctors. Although he might give advice of a general nature, Gillespie/ Zorba is most concerned with the development of the young professional. As such he represents the proper mixture of compassion and skill, emotional concern and trained competence. If the younger man risks too much to his unfinished skill because of an emotional involvement with a patient, it is the older man who calls his attention to the possible consequences of such attachments. If the student demonstrates a lack of human concern in his attention to clear physical danger, it is the older figure who teaches him to temper his professionalism. The "sons" are protected from the full consequences of their mistakes because these father/mentor figures hold positions of authority. When an unauthorized operation saves the life of a patient, the older man finds a way to overlook the technical and legal problems. The younger men are still likely to experience a severe reprimand which, considering its source, is doubtless more essential to their education than a formal inquiry into the matter. In spite of the prominent roles of the older men, the younger doctors are the center of our attention. It is their development that intrigues us and that provides the dramatic focus of the series. Paralleling that focus is our attention to the essentially professional problems of the young men. Above all we see them as doctors in the process of development.

Similar patterns may be found in the evolution of the legal formula. "Perry Mason" is the thorough professional, concerned almost exclusively with crime. "The Defenders" changes the pattern again to one more familial in tone. A widowed father and his son are partners in a prestigious law firm. Their cases revolve primarily around social issues and concentrate on examinations of constitutional rights. While there is the sense of youth being tutored by the wise father, the show again falls on the side of professionalism. The issues are forced outward, dealing with the controversy in an abstract fashion. Although individual human beings are touched by the issues that are explored, it is with the intellectual concept of the law that we are concerned.

"Slattery's People" and "The Senator" repeat this pattern, shifting the focus to legislative activity. Again the issues predominate at the expense of deep human relationships. There is no development of team or family, and the crusading central characters, polished and cerebral, remain at some distance from the audience. Both shows, though highly acclaimed critically, were popular failures.

The legal formula comes nearer to its most recent and successful version with the creation of "The Young Lawyers" and "The Storefront Lawyers." In each series an older professional is charged with the responsibility of overseeing the work of young, activist attorneys. Among the younger members of the cast a strong group sense develops. Most of their professional activity is directed toward the more underprivileged, socially forgotten element in America. Still oriented toward the defense of democratic principles, like "The Defenders" and "The Senator," the emphasis now is on the victim rather than on the principle itself. No matter how deep the emotional involvement, however, the structure of the episodes always leads to the moment in the courtroom in which the legal principle is upheld. More importantly, each successful defense demonstrates the dedication and wisdom of the young attorneys; the older, advisory figure is inevitably forced to recognize his secondary importance in the face of the development of the younger members of his profession.

Marcus Welby and Owen Marshall shift many of these basic patterns. While retaining elements of the earlier formulas, the emphasis is changed. The newer version seems to express a wide cultural need, and their popularity seems to extend beyond the usual medical or legal factors. That popularity is best explained as part of the larger pattern of television value structures that has been developing through our examination of other formulas.

In a culture that seems at times to be fanatically devoted to youth, the new popular heroes of medicine and law are the older men. In the process of shifting formulaic patterns the emphasis on roles has been reversed. No longer are we primarily concerned with the awareness, skills, sensitivity, and compassion of the younger man, with the trials and education of a Kildare or Casey or "young lawyers." We are now more interested in what it is that the older man says to his young assistant, and with how he guides him. The younger men remain, and their roles are crucial to the formulas. At times we see new versions of the old plots in which the apprentices are tested, initiated into the wisdom of the more practiced men. But the test is no longer one framed essentially to measure the young man's humility and willingness to take advice. Now he is measured by how much he resembles the older man once the advice is taken, how closely he follows in the footsteps of the mentor. Welby's assistant, Steve Kiley, may be a popular favorite with much of the audience, and may frequently figure prominently in the action of an episode, but it is Welby who remains at the center of the series, serving as the model and measure for Kiley and numerous other younger characters who enter his world.

That centrality is the result of any number of factors, some of which seem to reside chiefly in the character, others that are more dependent on setting and action. In purely physical terms Welby and Marshall are both older men. Welby is reaching the upper limits of middle age; Marshall is slightly younger. Both men are widowers. Welby has a daughter who lives far from him and who appears on the show occasionally; Marshall has a daughter in preadolescence who appears regularly. Both men are in excellent health, and we frequently see them exercising or performing other physical activities which emphasize their condition. They dress conservatively, though with some attention to fashion. Their hair is conservatively styled, though neither man is closely trimmed. Both are gray. Generally, they demonstrate moderation, a lack of extreme in any direction.

Professionally each man demonstrates highest competence. "Keeping up" with new areas of their pro-

fessions is a continuing activity on each show, and we
frequently observe the men engaged in research, reading legal or medical journals as part of their relaxa-
tion. The result is that Marshall has been offered lec-
tureships at the law school of the local university and
that Welby, though a general practitioner, is almost
never confronted with a medical situation in which
he cannot provide an answer, either through research
or reference to a specialist friend.

These personal and professional abilities grow out
of an emotional attitude that is crucial to understanding the importance of these characters. Both men
exhibit, above all else, a quality of concern. While that
concern is grounded in the professional nature of each
formula—concern with healing and with justice—it
moves quickly into other areas: concern for the social
system that produces ignorance about disease and human rights, concern about individuals who find themselves caught in dilemmas of emotional or physical
danger. This attitude can translate into anger as well
as compassion or into love as well as professional care.
When his friend is the victim of the rapist's attack,
Marshall is incensed that the police would imply that
she was more guilty than the man, that she complied
rather than suffer his actions. He is equally incensed
at the resulting silence on the part of other victims
and at the social attitude that makes such silence de-
fensible. He speculates about the number of unre-
ported rapes and suggests that if all of these were
reported, society would be forced to move quickly to
erase the discriminatory nature of its treatment of the
problem. When a young man is found to be suffering
from venereal disease, Welby is quick to comment on
the young man's actions, but his major concern is with
the ignorance that allows a social disease to per-

petuate itself. In guiding the young man to admit other relationships we see his concern expressed for those he is trying to protect as well as for those he is trying to heal.

Ultimately, these qualities refine themselves and combine into an essential stability. These men are trustworthy. They are, as expected, competent. Beyond that they are not separated from their clients and patients by professional pride, by expense, by moral sanctity, or by lack of compassion. They exhibit all the necessary qualities of superior fathers and are willing to take on significantly larger families than those we found in domestic comedy. Again, theirs are the values of an older time. In some ways they are the stock popular figures of country doctors and county seat lawyers. They are updated with all the advantages of science, research, movement, and ability.

Their immediate families are the teams of assistants who aid them in a professional and personal capacity. Both men have young assistants, and the relationship established with them, like that of the earlier formula prototypes, is of father and son. The younger men learn from the older, and on occasion, as with all "good" fathers, the older men are forced to admit that they learn from the younger as well. The most crucial aspect of this relationship is found in the fact that the two young men have chosen specific forms of their profession when they chose to practice with these particular older men. The distinction is more obvious in the medical show, where Kiley has given up a promising residency in neurosurgery in order to become a G.P. In the legal profession, where such distinctions are not as clear, there is still a choice implied in working with the private, individual lawyer rather than with a large corporation or a criminal law firm.

Like all father figures, the older men represent a whole way of life. The younger men learn to practice a different sort of law or medicine, but they also learn that such a choice carries with it choices about how to deal with people, about personal commitment, about a lack of luxury and its corresponding rewards in other areas. Most importantly, they learn about the order of priorities and concern. They are constantly being tested by the men with whom they work. Their highest reward is a judgment comparing them with the model, or a word from the model himself acknowledging the excellence of a particular performance.

In the cast of each show there is also a woman assistant. In the one she is a nurse-receptionist, in the other a specialized legal secretary. Both roles are important in that they reinforce the family quality by adding a subordinate feminine position for the cast. As usual the roles are firmly stereotyped and the women add warmth, feminine concern, and a lower level of professional competence. They become the firm but gentle mother-corrector. They are called on to point out the essentially loving relationship between the two men when it appears that they have irreconcilable differences. Marshall also has a young daughter who appears in his series. Her function is critical and compares with the function of very young children in the domestic comedy. Marshall is frequently placed in the position of having to explain to her the nature of his cases, and in the course of the explanations often realizes what his own stake in the situation is.

The impact of the cases handled by the professionals clearly affects the people who immediately

surround them. Those cases, however, the content of
the episodes, come from the outside, from a much
larger world. In the domestic comedy our attention,
even when attracted by outside events, is clearly focused on internal consequences. How will the family
react? What will be learned? How will the father in-
struct the children? Similarly, in the earlier forms of
the medical and legal dramas, we were concerned
with the growth of the younger member of the team.
The same questions could apply, but the action in the
new medical and legal formulas is directed outward.
The team of older and younger professionals moves to
problems beyond these immediate internal relationships. The medical and legal professions are by nature
social professions, directed toward serving other individuals. As a consequence, we now enter a world
fully populated by a well-developed supporting cast
which changes from week to week. The characters
in this cast are fictional representations of a "real"
world.

Such characters are not merely catalysts for action
to be performed by the central figures. They are fully
developed and their problems are rooted in complex
situations. Because of this, we care about them and
see them as central characters even though they will
not return for the next episode. They are central because, like the audience, they are willing to entrust
their problems—legal, physical, or emotional—to the
characters in whom the series are embodied. In a
sense, then, these characters become part of the larger
family that is ministered to by the professionals.

We are never allowed to forget that the primary
function of the central characters, healing and protecting, is carried on in settings that provide naturally
dramatic contexts for the solving of problems. The

operating room and the courtroom remind us of the archetypal problem of life versus death. The doctor is concerned with protecting innocent people from the random hand of disease, and the lawyer must protect the innocent from the more malevolent threat of unjust punishment. These rooms provide an arena in which to test the professional skill of the protectors, and many of the most crucial moments of television drama take place there. In almost every case, however, that traditional moment of tension and release is now subordinated to settings that link the doctors and lawyers to their more familial role.

Nothing is more important in this respect than the fact that both Welby and Marshall locate their offices in their homes. The houses themselves firmly define part of their dual function. Marshall's home is the more elaborate of the two, offering private space for his daughter to make a home and professional space for his associates. Welby's home is more modest, a frame and stone house. He and Kiley both live there, and though their quarters are comfortable, the larger portion of the house is given over to offices and examination rooms. Because they are not located in legal or medical centers, the doctor and lawyer must now move about. Welby still makes house calls, and we frequently follow him on excursions to visit older patients or those recently released from hospital. Such movement enlarges the world of the doctor or lawyer. Getting out of the hospital or courtroom makes it possible to get into any number of other worlds. The two characters and their associates are involved with persons from all other professions and social classes. It is this sense of a larger world that leads to the action of the shows, opening them up to problems that transcend the traditional medical or legal issue common to the previous versions of the formulas.

Our doctors and lawyers are privileged characters. They move with facility into the lives of a wide range of characters, the "lives" of the people who live near them. As they approach those lives in order to heal sickness, to protect from illegal harm, they move deeply into the more private areas as well. In doing so they minister to much more than the physical or social body of individuals. In their actions we see the development of a sort of popular formula combining many of the elements we have established as working elements of television.

Owen is asked to defend a young woman, a prospect for the Olympic diving team, from charges of professionalism which would bar her from competition. He interviews the girl and is moved by her desire to compete, her dedication to the ideals that would prevent the charges from being true. His assistant interviews her trainer-coach and is convinced of the same feeling. The charges, then, appear to be false and they agree to take the case. On the steps of the country club Marshall meets the woman who brought the charges accompanied by her husband. They are wealthy and handsome, and their congenial attitude indicates that they were not motivated by malice in bringing charges against Owen's client. When he informs them that he feels his case to be a strong one and that the girl will be allowed to compete, the woman becomes emotionally distraught. She informs her husband and Owen that she brought the professionalism charge to hide a more serious matter. She asserts that the girl attempted to seduce her young daughter and that she does not want the diver to become a model for young people.

Clearly the matter is serious, and Owen confronts his client with the new charges. Her response is one of unbelief and outrage. She recognized that the young girl was fond of her and produces a letter written by the child after the supposed seduction attempt. It expresses continuing affection for the older girl and given its date, could indicate that the story is a fabrication. When presented with this evidence, the younger girl says simply that it was written a year earlier. Because the envelope is lost, there is no way to dispute her story. A hearing begins, and as the young girl recounts the seduction scene the camera moves away and the personal details are not recounted to the audience.

We are allowed to hear the testimony of another prosecution witness, however, that of a former roommate of the accused. Under pressure she admits to writing a column for an underground newspaper devoted to homosexual liberation. She also admits to her own homosexuality but testifies that her relationship with the accused never reached an intimate level. The implication of guilt by association remains, and there is still no evidence to disprove the child's assertions.

The evidence comes when Owen establishes the earlier date for the letter by reference to a drawing in the letterhead. The drawing contains a picture of a recent addition to the hotel in which the people were staying and proves that the letter was written after the alleged seduction. On further questioning the young girl breaks into tears and admits that her entire story was false, created in order to regain the attention of the older girl, who she felt no longer cared for her. Her mother, she points out, is presently concerned with a new baby and pays little attention to her. "I am a person," she cries. "I exist,

I exist." Both the accused girl and the mother rush to the witness stand to comfort the child, but as the mother speaks encouragingly to her daughter, the older girl moves away, leaving them together.

Adding to the complexity of this episode are several other factors focusing on other characters. In a private conversation with her father, Marshall's daughter reminds him of a report she has done on Tchaikovsky and of her own knowledge of homosexuality. In a conversation between Owen's assistant and secretary the young woman recalls whispers she caused by stating in a high school class that her ambition was to become the first woman Supreme Court Justice. The testimony of the lesbian witness adds yet another factor when she admits that she is not ashamed of what she is. All these items, when placed in proper artistic context as portions of the action of the episode, add special dimensions. Clearly, Owen Marshall's practice is involved with more than legal intricacies.

Compare Marshall's case, now, with one of Welby's. A friend of Steve Kiley's comes to the clinic for examination. His tests confirm his own suspicions of radiation sickness caused by a laboratory accident some years earlier. The disease is in the critical stages, and the young man is prepared to die, hoping only to complete a major book on which he is working. Welby, Kiley, and a specialist, however, agree that a bone marrow transplant might save the man's life. The only donor available is the man's retarded brother. The parents of the two men feel that it would be unfair to "use" their other son in this way. The patient is guilty about it himself. Adding to his feeling is the fact that he once tried to set a broken arm for his brother which resulted in great pain when the arm was reset. Since that time the retarded man has been severely frightened by doctors, by the thought of pain such as would be caused by an operation.

Welby talks with the younger man, and then convinces the parents that though he is mentally retarded, he is emotionally sound and wishes to help his brother. In a highly emotional scene the younger brother convinces the older that he wants to help because of his love. The operation is performed, is successful. The younger man functions more fully having re-established a loving relationship with all his family and having won their respect because of his actions. The entire family is grateful to Welby for making it all possible.

The complexities of such episodes indicate clearly that Welby, Marshall, and other characters like them are protecting and healing on many levels. In the most simple sense the essential problems created by medical and legal formats have been solved; Welby's patient has been healed and Marshall's client cleared of unjust charges and protected from prosecution. If we take such actions as central, the circles of influence and activity begin immediately to spread into other areas.

Welby's patient has not simply been healed of his physical sickness. Because of his doctor's skill at detecting emotional illness, he has been guided into a new relationship with his family. His inability to accept his brother's affliction had acted as a tumor, eating away at his ability to care for other people. That illness is now cured. Similarly, Marshall's client, in a moment of conversation, admits that her life-style affords ample opportunity for suspicion on the part of those so inclined. Her athletic activity has consumed her life, blocking off "normal" relationships such as dating, group activity, adolescent "fun." Having come to this realization, there is no longer any need for the situation to continue and she plans to change.

On another level we must notice that both shows involve us directly with the problems of families once again. Though the family members are no longer the central characters of the continuing series, their problems form central conflicts for the shows. Marshall's client would not have come under suspicion had the mother not cared for her daughter. But the daughter would not have created the lie had her relationship with her parents been more stable, more complete. It is this family problem that Marshall has ultimately alleviated. For Welby, the problem is to bring the family to the realization that love means not only protection and isolation of the retarded brother but acceptance of his individuality as well. In the final scene of the episode Welby stands with the father and mother of the retarded man and they watch as he runs to the bus that carries him, with those like him, to the training center. His whole attitude has been changed by the fact that his family has allowed him to participate, to help, in their lives. Their lives are equally richer for the experience.

Because of their professional capacities, Welby and Marshall have been allowed to enter these family lives as counselors and guides. They have established their compassion and concern again and again, and they are able to stand aside and probe relationships, touch the weaknesses, the emotional illnesses, of the people with whom they deal. The patients and clients hesitate at first, unsure of the motives and abilities of these men. Such people are locked into their own lives. Finally, the families recognize that the goodness and the skill, factors they are willing to accept at the professional level, extend into the more private areas as well.

The audience has been waiting for such acceptance because it has known all along that such central characters are ultimately to be trusted with the deepest problems these other characters may have. The audience knows this because a carefully structured relationship has been created between it and the "world" of television drama. Part of the relationship has to do with the larger outlines of television entertainment. There is never any question that in a show of this type the essential problem will be solved. Such expectations are not allowed because the show must continue and the star must continue to be the central character. In medical and legal terms this means that the patient must survive and that the client must be acquitted in order for the star to prove his reason for being. It also means that the more emotional problem, which has become the central focus for the plot, will be solved as well. We have come to trust the counseling function of these professionals just as we trust their more technical functions.

Increasingly we have come also to expect some sort of knowledge, some information, that is directed toward the audience and that increases our belief that these men know what they are talking about and are to be trusted. Every episode of Owen Marshall or Marcus Welby contains a strong "informational" component. In Marshall's homosexuality case we learn explicitly what it means to be a homosexual in American society. We learn of the pain caused by public inacceptance of private morality and of the deception that results from it. We learn, too, that there are individuals who are not ashamed of their sexual preferences and that there is a movement to change the social attitude. In the rape case we listen as Owen passionately quotes lists of statistics proving that rape is the most common violent crime in our society. Such statistics are verifiable if the audience so desires. When Welby tours the training center for retarded adults, we do not see actors portraying patients and teachers. We see real persons, as in the past we have seen real agencies operating to aid emotionally disturbed children, deaf children, physically handicapped adults, and so on. The "real" reality is structured into each show, offering the audience information and guidance for its own possible problems.

For every episode that touches a correctable physical or social ill also touches human beings. In an important sense the information and healing and counseling offered by the lawyers and doctors in a professional area are the easiest part of their job. The tough problems solved by Welby and Marshall are the problems of those who must care for the socially, mentally, and physically handicapped. How does one accept a handicapped child? How does one live with one's failures as a parent? How does one accept death? When our counselors and confessors help their fictional characters solve these problems, as they always do, they are again directing advice toward the audience.

Such advice embodies traditional American values, and in structuring these shows television is openly and explicitly didactic. If our society, our culture, offers only a relativistic morality, then we can turn on the television set to see problems worked out for us in terms of a simpler set of shared values. There we are called on to care for each other, to accept emotional disability as we would accept physical pain. The doctors and lawyers speak to their young assistants, teaching them how to perform their professional services in the most acceptable moral way. They speak to their clients and patients, helping them to come to terms with the difficulties in their lives, healing the broken family structures they find. They speak to their audience perhaps not as fathers, but as advising uncles, removed from us by a fictional frame, related to us by the content within that frame.

They are less concerned with elemental violence than is the traditional Western or mystery hero. They are more able to deal with contemporary problems than those heroes because doing so does not strain our belief in the traditional roles. But finally, they are quite similar to those other characters and to the all-wise fathers of situation and domestic comedy. Our problems, like our illnesses, are not always cured by wise and compassionate individuals. If television creates for us a set of values for living, it also creates the illusion that our lives can be made whole within a sixty-minute time slot—interrupted only by eight minutes of commercial message. When that standardized frame is broken, we find ourselves moving, although only slightly, toward a different sort of television art.

6

ADVENTURE SHOWS: LONERS, FUGITIVES, AND EXPLORERS

The idea of conflict is central to much popular art. We expect our heroes to be tested, and often the strength of our reaffirmation depends on the degree of physical combat, psychic stress, or spiritual agony involved in his ordeals. The mystery begins with murder and takes us through a series of near-misses, solid hits, and newly discovered bodies. The Western entices us with the unknown events beyond the horizon or the unrevealed speed of the gunfighter's draw. Doctors and lawyers battle death, injustice, and emotional difficulty. All melodrama depends on a structure that sees the central characters as threatened, and even the mildest situation comedy or farce frequently depends on a slapstick version of cliff-hanging danger or on a parody of the chase-capture-escape motif. In some of these versions conflict is equated with violence. Each week the hero must put his own life on the line in order to "protect" his constituency, and in order to prevent his own death he might be called on at any moment to kill. Surrounding these central lines of plot are all the trappings of "adventure." Mysterious characters, exotic locations, cryptic messages, dark streets, and the skills of battle assure us that our entertainment will move out of the "normal" world of mundane experience. Even the nightly news will be criticized for failing to thrill, and a peaceful day without major tension or disaster will hardly make "good" news.

Though all these forms involve us in exciting action or titillate us with the prospect of the hero's demise, none of them can be most effectively defined as an adventure show. In all of them the idea of adventure is confined by the structures that make use of it but that subordinate it to the meanings emerging more directly from standard and repeatable characters and content.

There is another set of shows, however, in which this process works in the opposite direction. Certain factors link them with mysteries or Westerns. The central characters of "Route 66" or of "Run for Your Life" may find themselves involved in the same kind of personal entanglement that provides the focus for many episodes of "Marcus Welby." Richard Kimball, better known as the title character of "The Fugitive," finds his life determined by his connection in a murder case. "Star Trek" is science fiction, and that means that the characters are able to discover many roles, among them those of detectives or cowboys. Finally, however, these shows and others like them cannot be placed with those other formulas that they resemble. In some ways the television adventure formula, then, makes it possible to link television with other forms of art and makes possible the increasingly complex development of the medium itself.

The first defining characteristic of the formula is movement. Episodes begin when the central characters arrive on the scene; they end when the action is finished and the characters leave. Buzz and Todd crisscross the country in a random pattern on "Route 66." Kimball stays on the move. The crew of the starship *Enterprise* continues to explore the reaches of time and space. Again, this is not a characteristic limited to use on adventure shows. Characters in other types of series can move about freely as well. Often we find an episode of "Ironside" structured around the idea that the detective and his associates are vacationing in the mountains or visiting old friends in Canada. Some types of Western are premised on the wagon train moving West or on the cattle drive. We have just discussed the ways in which Marshall and Welby must move about in their communities.

The factor that distinguishes the two kinds of movement and that goes a step further in defining the adventure formula is motivation. When Ironside visits a little fishing village somewhere north of San Francisco, he goes there as "the detective on vacation." When McCloud goes to London or to Hawaii, he goes as "detective in search of clues" or as "representative of a police department." When the cattle drover or wagon master moves about, he is engaged in distinctively western undertakings. The movement is always dependent on roles that are fitted into existing formulas. The formulas define the roles—detective, cowboy—and the formula makes possible the occasional movement.

For characters in adventure series the motivation is the result of character rather than of role. Role is a function of formula. Motivations rise from a required set of actions and events. Audience expectations are shaped by the strict limitations in which the roles are defined. Characters approach the status of invention, their motivations are internal, and the audience is willing to wait and see what happens in the course of events. The adventure series quickly makes a role of the internally motivated character, of course. The Fugitive must always leave the scene of his current involvement before he is captured. But during the episode he has behaved as a complex human being, torn between his "role" as imposed within this formula and his own feelings, which are the ones that motivate his adventure. Similarly, the crew of the *Enterprise* are given roles by the science fiction structure in which they exist, but science fiction series offer special possibilities within which to develop character, and most of the action of the series rises from interaction among thoroughly defined characters. For Buzz and Todd the structure is less defined than in either of the other series. They simply wander. As they do they portray contemporary characters who are given no role other than those that they create in the various episodes and that develop continuity over a period of time.

What this means is that the content of any given episode of an adventure series is not restricted to a certain type of encounter. The adventures are random, and other characters move in and out of the lives of the central figures. Again, the distinction between this type of encounter and that experienced on other series lies in the minimal restriction of the adventure formula. For example, we frequently see good television acting on a show such as "Marcus Welby," because the formula allows for individual character development. Because the show is somewhat flexible in format, the events of one episode do not necessarily resemble those of another in specific detail. From one point of view, then, the central characters interact with a new set of supporting characters each week, and we see into all sorts of lives as a result. But the formulaic structure is rigid, and we know that the characters who enter Welby's life will have a medical problem that will be linked to some sort of personal or emotional problems and that the task for the doctor is the healing of both. In the more traditional formulas the rigidity is even more complete. Only certain types of events may occur in the mystery and Western formulas. If these types are willing to subordinate the traditional events to television events, concentrating on contemporary social problems, they still must resolve the problems in the traditional manner.

For the adventure series no such restrictions exist. Following our characters, we may find ourselves in a mystery one week only to be involved in a spy story the next. In special cases it is even possible for the characters to become involved in what would be defined as western action. Frequently these plots fall back on traditional motifs of excitement and tension. With only a first-aid manual the heroes must remove an appendix. For variation, they become involved in the delivery of a baby under primitive conditions. Episodes see them interacting with runaway children, with marital problems, with amnesia victims, or in the more action-oriented series, with entrapments, showdowns, hand-to-hand battles. But none of these things need occur in the following week, for we may be a thousand miles from the scene. Nor will there be a continuing set of supporting characters, a familiar location, or a set of professional expectations. There will be only movement and new encounter.

The unspecified action of the adventure series, then, may be creative or repetitive. In either case the pattern follows that of the television hour, and particular problems are solved by the time the episode is concluded. They are not solved in terms of formulaic structures such as the Western, or in terms of predetermined roles such as the country doctor, however, but in terms of values embodied in the central characters. Values that determine the outcomes of various encounters are directly related to the attitudes that motivate the movement of the characters in the first place. The values that make it necessary for the characters to move are those that prevent their lives from becoming formulaic, their personalities from becoming roles. There are many reasons for "moving on." The series are constructed around those various motives.

"Route 66" presents a television version of that old and powerful American dream, the wanderer as hero. So much of our cultural experience is defined by the image of the youth in search of something vague, something that can be found only in multiple experiences. Benjamin Franklin wandered from Boston to Philadelphia, was stranded on the river, and spent his last pennies for those great puffy rolls long before he reinterpreted it all into something normal and expected. Thoreau on the shore of Walden created an inward journey as exciting as any fictional narrative and suggested the virtues of physical travel into more remote areas in search of "wildness." Ishmael and his counterparts "went to sea" in an almost ritualistic exercise in freedom. Natty Bumppo moved continually just beyond the frontier and in doing so prepared the way for explorers and trappers, mountain men, and ultimately for the cowboy. After the close of the frontier the cowboy became the most potent expression of our wandering spirit, and the tightening grip of history and geography can be closely correlated with the rise of the cowboy's image in the popular arts. But the television cowboy is too domesticated and too remote in experience. Tied to a town or to a role, his freedom is restricted and he represents a period more than an idea.

In 1955, with the publication of Jack Kerouac's *On*

the Road, the dream awakened again. The novel describes a part of a generation that cannot continue to accept the values of America in mid-twentieth century. The expatriate experience of the twenties is sterile for them. The "beatniks" set out to re-enact the movement of the settlers, to rediscover America, to look underneath the settled middle classes, to go on the road. They are depicted as haunted, frustrated, excitable, and bored—individuals who find adventure in their wandering, their search. They have no destination beyond a vague notion of "experience." They are the antithesis of America's love of stability and order. They reject the admonition to settle and build. Structure and predictability, regimen and continuity are anathema to Kerouac's characters.

In "Route 66" we see the middle-class version of the anti-middle-class dream. The loners are laundered and polished, made safe for the mass audience. Todd and Buzz are neat, their hair short and clean. They do not grow beards or wear sandals; their sunglasses are functional rather than symbolic of their cynicism. Their intake of wine never approaches the excesses of Kerouac's hipsters. Though they may fall in love in a given episode or encounter the problems of a drug addict in another, they reject the idea that drugs and sex are essential to the meaning of life.

Despite the differences between them, Buzz and Todd, on the one hand, and the beatniks on the other are seeking the same sort of abstract experience. The rule for loners is that it is good to get experience, to wander in search of it. It is good not to be tied down. It is good to be able to leave situations and people, even though the ties to the people are sometimes strong. Freedom is the key. In a way these young men seem to express the opposite vision from that found in domestic comedy. There, the virtues of home, school, family, and career are extolled by wise fathers. Occasionally the fathers recognize that their sons should engage in a bit of wandering and might even confess to some wild moments in their own younger days. Ultimately we always come back to the lesson learned, that the point of wandering is the discovery of home. This is not the case in "Route 66."

The primary values embodied in the show are those of the loner. Motivation is left at this vague level, for the loner is moving toward no goal, is seeking nothing in particular. Youth is a prime ingredient, and there is a continual tension between these days of wandering and some future time when such a life may be impossible. We cannot imagine two fifty-five-year-old "loners."

The loner must be exceptionally open to new experience and as a consequence, must be able to accept values and attitudes other than his own. When problems are solved, then, it is with this primary openness at the center of the action. Buzz and Todd cannot afford to judge on the basis of some predetermined morality or according to the rules of a code. They cannot behave as detectives or cowboys who have many unwritten rules by which to measure the characters with whom they come into contact. The loner is compassionate, willing to be friends with all classes and all occupations. He enters their problems, and the reflection of their various stations in society in those problems is part of the search for experience. Thus Todd and Buzz become involved with shrimp fishermen in Biloxi and steel workers in Pittsburgh as well as with the children of the rich who hitch rides along the highways. The point is that while they accept all of these people, all of these lives, as equally valid, they refuse to become bound or restricted by any of them.

The most pervasive symbol of this series, the one that defines the attitude toward the wanderer's dream and the middle-class response to it, is the automobile. The gleaming, chunky Corvette in which Buzz and Todd roam the country is the key to freedom, to movement, to getting away. It is the cowboy's horse, the hitchhiker's thumb, the boxcar of the thirties. If the boys have to stop at times and take jobs in order to earn gas money, still there are no wives, children, mortgages, or careers to hold them there. Additionally, during their stops, many of their adventures occur. The sports car is daring; it holds only two. It moves swiftly and is designed more for speed than for safety.

Obviously, such an automobile, or for that matter, any automobile, is repulsive to the beatnik. To the viewer of "Route 66" each Friday night, it is the mediator between the wonderful world of adventure and his own, more mundane life. He can take his family for a Sunday drive and imagine that he is "on the road." If his car is the typical family-oriented four-door sedan, he can see it as a covered wagon rather than the wild pony of the cowboy. The automobile is still the symbol of open land in a frontierless America. If the Sunday driver tunes his radio to a station playing the theme music from "Route 66," a popular hit, he may have to be wakened from his dreams by his wife in order to return home in time for "The Ed Sullivan Show." "Route 66" was sponsored by Chevrolet, and no doubt, the sales of Corvettes increased because of it.

As loners Todd and Buzz come to us as mythic travelers. They have no history. They seem to have no personal attachments to people other than those whom they meet in their journey. They have a fierce loyalty to one another, and at times threats to this relationship serve as the central theme of an episode. But they always manage to stay together. This friendship, the shared belief in the value of wandering, in the gathering of experience, is the only destination they seem to have. They are certainly heading for no definable geographic spot. They are not searching for purpose, for the purpose is in the wandering itself.

This is not the case with "The Fugitive" and its imitators. The opening shots of "Route 66" offer us a montage of road signs, movement, the gleaming Corvette speeding down an open road. The opening shots of "The Fugitive" ground us in a world of harsh reality, a world in which history is a huge social and personal thing. The format of the title shots has varied through the years, but it always manages quickly to recount a complex series of events on which the show is premised.

We open as Dr. Richard Kimball is driving toward his home in a fashionable suburb. As he approaches his drive, a man darts from the yard and Kimball is forced to brake sharply in order to avoid striking him. As the car dips to a halt, he notices that the man seems to be panicked, to be fleeing from Kimball's house. The man is dressed as a vagrant, and as he turns to face the car that has almost hit him, we see that he has only one arm. Kimball then hurries into his house and finds it in a state of disorder that indicates a struggle. Then he discovers the body of his murdered wife. He is tried and convicted of the murder on circumstantial evidence. No one can discover the one-armed man and no one else seems to have seen him. Those who try Kimball believe that he has fabricated the entire episode. As he is being transported to the state prison, the train on which he is riding is wrecked. The detective who is accompanying him is knocked unconscious. Kimball is able to free himself and run. It is not coincidental that his panic, his frightened manner, resembles that of the one-armed man he had seen weeks earlier. The narrator now tells us that fate has made of Dr. Richard Kimball—the Fugitive.

Visually all this information is presented much more succinctly than it can be summarized, and the audience is thoroughly familiar with the events. Yet they are recounted each week, and frequently individual episodes recapitulate certain key details in Kimball's history. These opening scenes and recapitulations are less important as information, however, than as part of the structure of the series. As part of the strict formula of "The Fugitive" they serve as a frame that continually comments on and modifies the meaning of the events of a given episode. Each week's story begins with the retold history, the chain of events that forced the fugitive to run. Some versions of the opening sequence conclude with a helicopter shot in which the camera moves farther and farther away from Kimball, who is hurrying from the train wreck. In later, more stylized versions, still photographs are used to tell the entire story, and in a final frame the camera zooms in on Kimball as he attempts to break loose the dangling handcuff that is attached to his wrist. In either version the narrator introduces the idea of fate, and Kimball becomes a toy for larger controlling forces. The forces become increasingly apparent and frightening.

From this historically based opening, each episode then moves into the second segment. Here we discover Kimball in the current situation. We may see him stepping off a bus, asking for a job, accepting a ride as a hitchhiker. Or we may discover that he is well established in an occupation. Usually his work involves hard labor, and at all costs he must avoid disclosing his identity as a doctor. In the third segment a complication arises. He falls in love, perhaps, or is recognized by a traveler. He may rescue a drowning child and refuse to have his picture placed in the local newspaper, arousing the suspicion of the editor. In any case the complication forces him to confront his past. The woman he now loves may wish to marry, but feels that she needs to know more about him before she makes a decision. His picture may appear in the newspaper despite his wishes. Somehow, the events that took place years ago and that made him a fugitive always come back. In the fourth segment the complication is heightened. As a result, he must become evasive, mysterious, deceptive, in order to avoid a probe into his life. In the fifth segment he is forced to choose between life as he has found it, has come to enjoy it, and life as a fugitive. If he chooses to maintain his new life, he will be discovered. In almost every episode this segment produces tension as the pursuing detective draws nearer. Finally, in the closing moments of the episode, Kimball chooses once again to flee, to give up his new life and new identity in order to maintain his fugitive state. As the show ends, the frame that opened with the retold history closes as Kimball hops a train, thumbs a ride, or hides in the bushes as the siren of a police car brings his pursuer to the scene, inevitably a moment too late.

Like Todd and Buzz, Kimball leaves behind him people whose lives are made better by his presence. But in his case this is the result of a more complex interaction. On "Route 66" the freedom exemplified in the young men's way of life is frequently a liberating force. Sometimes people are more able to see the emptiness of their own lives after meeting these two loners who have rejected many socially accepted values. Even more often, they see themselves living with unwanted or unneeded restrictions. Being able to go "on the road" is an expression of freedom chosen over other sorts of lives. "The Fugitive" represents no such freedom. His wandering is forced upon him and he lives outside the law. His life, then, is far more restricted than the lives of those he meets while wandering. He envies them. Given the choice, he would gladly exchange the life of the wanderer for a home, a family, a career—all the things that are snatched from him by circumstance.

In this way "The Fugitive" uses the wandering adventurer motif as a means of reaffirming social values rather than for calling them into question. Yet in this reaffirmation lies the central paradox of the formula and a factor that is a key in the popularity of the series. To gain the freedom to have the things he wants, the fugitive must submit to the much greater restriction of injustice. The audience knows that he did not murder his wife from those opening frames. Yet he can live a "normal" life only if he is willing to return and face imprisonment, the term of which will now be extended because of his continual flight from the authorities. His only hope, of course, is to solve the mystery of his wife's murder, to find the one-armed man. In this structure the relentless police lieutenant who pursues him becomes the villain, unwilling to admit the innocence of the fugitive. The producers of the series continually emphasize the contrasting values of the two men. The policeman's strict interpreta-

tion of the law and the fugitive's humane consideration of all those he meets are carefully pointed out
for us as the two men are occasionally brought together for a few minutes. Each time the policeman
is forced to admit the "goodness" of the man he
pursues. Perhaps he sees him care for an injured person. At least once the fugitive saves the life of the
policeman, and it is obvious that he allows Kimball
to escape. Increasingly, through the years of the
series, the fugitive, the policeman, and the audience
are forced to question the validity of a system that
so obviously restrains and persecutes an individual.

From the opening scenes throughout the tight-wire
suspense to the final escape the emphasis of the episode is on the idea of fate, the excruciating play of
coincidence in Kimball's perpetual flight. In a very
real sense he does not fight the law or the social forces
that push him around. Like the detective who pursues
him despite an increasing reluctance, like the people
whom he accidentally encounters, Kimball is the
object of forces much larger than himself. But each
week he manages to fight this fate and win. Each time
he avoids capture, he has symbolically avoided suc-
cumbing to the forces over which he has so little
control. His freedom from the law is an expression of
human freedom. In this way his struggle is more complex than that of the detective or the cowboy. These
figures have their codes, they know their enemies,
whereas Kimball's flight expresses a continuing American tension between a need for authority on the one
hand and a fear of totalitarianism on the other.

This fugitive version of the adventure formula is
easily translatable into other situations. One of these,
"The Invaders," was only moderately successful. At
the center of the situation was an individual who had

definite knowledge that Martian invaders were in the process of taking over the earth. Because the Martians could assume human forms, however, and because they disappeared when killed, he could never convince the authorities of his reliability. In an effort to discredit him the Martians repeatedly set up events through which he would be blamed for crimes and sought by the authorities. In each episode he managed to convince a few individuals of the truth of his information, but there was none of the continuing sense of history that so fully controlled "The Fugitive." The show could be seen as an attempt to translate "The Fugitive" comment on the human condition into political terms. Martians attempting to invade the earth could just as easily be political enemies of the state. In any case, the show died quickly.

A more successful version was "Run for Your Life." In many ways this series represents a combination of the ideas of "Route 66" and "The Fugitive." Paul Bryan, the central character, like Richard Kimball, is a condemned man. His sentence, however, has been passed by a doctor rather than by a court. He has been told that he is to die. He may have three years, he may have six months. At any rate his future is drastically shortened and he knows it. Having received this notice, Paul, like Buzz and Todd, decides on a life of wandering. He plans to cram all the experiences of life into whatever time he has left. The opening shots again tell the story each week as we see him skydiving, exploring, and in the central image of the titles, driving a race car at top speed along what appears to be a speed test track. The shot is from the driver's perspective and the center line which is to guide the car wavers beneath its nose. It seems to be heading somewhere, but the end point is lost in the distance. There is only the movement, the excessive speed.

Paul's adventures, like those of Kimball, Buzz, and Todd, are totally random. Each week he comes into contact with other individuals and may find himself involved in a spy story, a mystery, a domestic problem story, or occasionally a comedy. Like the other wanderers, he helps these people and generally manages to solve their problems. He is not forced to hide his identity as is Kimball, and he moves about in the most open manner, visiting the glamour spots of Europe, exotic out-of-the-way islands, the great cities of America and the small towns. Frequently he meets old acquaintances. In these situations something comparable to the strain of "The Fugitive" is brought into the circumstances, for Paul does not wish to share his knowledge of imminent death with his friends, nor does he wish to cause undue tension in the relationships. It does, however, for the audience knows that he is frequently embarrassed by mention of the future, by requests to make plans. The audience also knows that he can establish no lasting relationships, make no home, build no career. As with Kimball it is not a case of rejecting those values. Again it is a case of fate refusing to let the man have what he wants. Paul is much freer than most of the audience —rich, traveled, cultured. But the idea of his death reverses the situation. He is condemned and we are the ones who are free. This is an ironic reaffirmation of all that the audience is supposed to believe in. But those accepted values are held in tension with the dream of ultimate freedom. His ability to put these two dreams into perspective allows Paul to deal humanely with all those whom he meets. Such a show offers the most complex examination of human values that we have yet dealt with.

In its own time "Run for Your Life" offered a rare television comment on the problem of existence. Though Paul did not, and could not, die in any of his adventurous exploits, the possibility was there. It was not the subject matter of the show, and there were no complex philosophical explorations of the theme. But embedded in the structure of an apparently typical adventure show this idea served to frame formulaic television events.

The third type of formula that qualifies as "adventure" is the science fiction series. The sci-fi anthology, familiar from the days of "Twilight Zone," does not qualify here, for it does not make possible a continuation of central characters or a major premise that will allow for wandering. The answer to both these problems is found in shows such as "Voyage to the Bottom of the Sea," "Land of the Giants," "Lost in Space," and most famous of them all, "Star Trek."

"Voyage," while developing no real complexity in and of itself, does indicate quite clearly the way in which the science fiction formula can be developed into the adventure format. If the major assumption of the "Route 66" type of adventure is the encounter of the loner with new environments, and the premise of "The Fugitive" is indicated by the title, the basis of the science fiction series must be designated as that of the "explorer." Here, as in the two other types of adventure, the defining characteristic indicates the basic value structure of each episode.

The crew of the submarine *Seaview* is involved in a sort of perpetual underwater exploration. In the course of these voyages they encounter various types of antagonists. Because much of the action is restricted by the rather cramped and confining quarters of the submarine, many of the encounters involve "monsters" or terrible "beasts" that can grow and develop in an isolated laboratory or in some chamber in the depths of the boat's interior. These monsters are fantastic in all the sense developed in "monster" movies. Tiny fish grow to incredible size. Bits of seaweed become voracious, carnivorous plants. In such cases the audience comes to have ultimate faith in the crew's ability to devise some sort of deterrent, a net of electricity or atomic power, that will disintegrate the monster.

In a slightly more sophisticated version of the same theme the crew is forced to confront more subtle enemies. Spies are sometimes placed on board, or, more likely, mad scientists in the guise of well-meaning marine biologists infiltrate the group. In these cases it is necessary for the crew to react in a more complicated manner. At times this psychological threat is combined with the physical in plots that see crew members or command staff "inhabited" by the evil ideas of the antagonist. In these cases it may become necessary for a reluctant subordinate to "kill" his superior in order for the evil forces to release his body.

"Voyage to the Bottom of the Sea" begins, in these monstrous encounters, a pattern that is further developed by "Star Trek." In each of these encounters the first resort is to the massive technology represented by the submarine. In no case, however, is this a sufficient answer. In the explorer motif we must always fall back finally on the human beings involved. This may call for ingenuity, intuition, common sense, or such old-fashioned values as loyalty and obedience. In any case, this is what will save the day.

This same pattern is carried into "Land of the Giants," which manages to combine elements of several formulas in its own science fiction terms. The explorer motivation enters in two ways. First, the title shots capsulize a history in which a space shuttle containing the members of the cast is drawn off course, out of control, and is wrecked on an alien planet. Except for physical dimensions, the planet is an exact duplicate of earth. The environment is the same. Even the people appear in human form. The only difference is that the members of the cast are no bigger than tiny animals in comparison with the size of the environment and inhabitants of the new planet. From a beginning as space explorers, then, these people have become the explorers of a new earthlike environment. They are forced to live the primitive life of pioneers, and in their search for food, tools, and materials with which to repair their spaceship, for information on how to exist, they are continually confronted with difficult problems inherent in the relationship of their size in this new environment. They are Robinson Crusoes in the bodies of Tom Thumb. Somewhat to their dismay, they soon learn that they are also fugitives. The inhabitants of the planet are first terrified of their presence and later become intent on capturing them. There is even a persistent police captain who makes their capture and retention his passion. Additionally, there are all sorts of scientists who want them for experiments, children who want them for pets, or self-serving mercenaries who want them for a reward which is placed on their heads.

Much more than in "Voyage," the complexities of "Land of the Giants" are involved with problems that mirror the problems of our own world. In the first place the cast is mixed in terms of age, race, sex, and moral attitude. From the white male hero captain, through his black assistant and female stewardesses, to the child and his dog, to the corrupt public official fleeing with embezzled money, we are supposed to see a spectrum of beliefs and attitudes. The interaction of these characters can involve plots that range from the sentimental complication of the boy's near loss of his dog to the exploration of greed as a basic human emotion.

The second factor that allows examination of contemporary problems is the suggestion that the alien planet is like earth. The little people frequently find themselves involved with the problems of the people who inhabit the planet. A drunk sleeping in a park awakes to find a body nearby, a gun in his hand. The little people happen to have seen the real murderer and through a series of contorted actions see to it that the innocent man is protected, the guilty man captured. A small boy, sadistically inclined because of the indulgence of his father, has caused a number of fires. The little people make his actions known and the father reforms.

In each episode both of these plot types are usually combined with more straightforward adventure plots in which the little people must fight for their lives in some way. Additionally, each episode sees some of them captured. The process of survival and exploration, the capture-escape theme, the exploration of their own motivations, and the probing of moral issues involving people who strongly resemble contemporary Americans are all combined in this mix. There is little sense of realism, however, and the show remains at the level of fantasy.

"Star Trek" represents the opposite end of the spectrum. It brings to television all the sophistication of

the science fiction novel, story, movie, and radio serial. That sophistication rests on the skill with which
the creators of science fiction can turn their future-
oriented tales into incisive tools with which to examine the world in which we live. Part of the skill is
dependent on the sense of functional probability;
while speculating wildly the artist of science fiction
works within the limits of available knowledge. His
task is to stretch that knowledge without breaking
it, to examine the thinking that underlies technological advancement. Frequently, it is the thought rather
than the advancement itself that becomes the center
of the fiction. Here, "Star Trek" spares no pains. Although individual episodes might depend on some
sort of outlandish encounter with an alien planet and
its inhabitants, the basic premises of the series, including the scientific premises, are carefully designed to
remain within the realm of probability. The design
of the starship *Enterprise* was completed with the aid
of experts in aerospace design. The theories of space
travel involving light speeds and time and the mech-
anisms necessary to achieve them were carefully
checked by physicists.

Even more important, perhaps, is the essential probability of character and event that underlies the show.
The "mission" of the *Enterprise,* we are told each
week, is to "boldly go where no man has gone before."
Space is designated as the final frontier, a factor that
becomes increasingly important. Into such a world
must come characters of a certain sort: brave, daring,
self-conscious, resourceful, at times a bit foolhardy,
they are best designated as explorers. These are the
characteristics of the true pioneer, and the people
are different from loners in that they have a highly
developed sense of purpose. They are different from

fugitives in that their purposes are affirmative and are the result of choice rather than chance. Their journeys have little to do with a mere accumulation of experience. Nor does fate toy with them. They find their meaning in a directed, selected mission. Over and over, this theme of identity in exploration is made clear. These people have chosen to sacrifice the comforts of home and family, but unlike the wanderers of "Route 66," they have become a part of the larger family of the crew.

This sense of family, or of interdependence, is fostered by two aspects of the show. The first is that the crew is multiracial and international. Additionally, a conscious effort has been made to include females in key, though subordinate positions. In this way "Star Trek" comments on the fragmented and prejudiced nature of our own societies and cultures. The second aspect is best illustrated by the much observed multiple personality of the command staff. The most prominent character is Mr. Spock, the half-human, half-Vulcan who serves as the chief science officer. He is noted for exhibiting the Vulcan trait of absolute allegiance to logic. He continually scores humans for their slavish attention to the emotional aspects of their natures. To this he attributes many of their personal faults as well as the faults of their cultures and societies. Because his mother was human, however, Spock is forced to admit occasionally that the emotions are valuable and can temper the colder regions of logic with a needed warmth. Opposite Spock is Dr. McCoy, the ship's physician. A Southerner by birth, he is tempestuous, excitable, and frequently angry. A third perspective is offered in Scotty, the chief engineer. He is mechanical and technological in his outlook. But he also represents the intuitive aspects of human nature, and often creates devices, modifies structures, and overrides systems in ways that work, though by Spock's calculations they are illogical and improbable.

All of these points of view are brought together and focused in the character of James T. Kirk, the captain of the *Enterprise*. In dealing with his responsibility for the ship, her mission, and her crew, Kirk is faced repeatedly with dilemmas that must be solved, and in most cases his choices for solutions demonstrate the folly of overlooking one or more of these life views. Kirk must continually learn the lesson that is implicit in the structure of his staff, that man must be whole in order to function best, to be most human.

The importance of this holistic human attitude is emphasized again in the pattern of action in most individual episodes. In the course of its cruises the *Enterprise* encounters some sort of problem. In some cases the problem is set up by a specific assignment: to explore an apparently barren planetoid, to visit a delegation from an alien civilization. On other occasions the ship simply encounters an unknown situation: other ships have been attacked, planets have been destroyed, an invasion force is moving toward them. On still other occasions strange things begin to happen aboard the ship: erratic behavior among members of the crew or the command staff, malfunction of some component of the ship. The first reaction to any of these problems, as in the other shows we have examined, is to rely on essentially technological methods to reach a successful conclusion. It becomes apparent, however, that such solutions are incapable of rectifying the situation, and once again human abilities, common sense, and human emotions bring about the correction.

This is so because most of the plots for the series ultimately rest on problems inherent in the human social condition. The need for mutual love and respect, the need for compassion, a recognition of the rather small role of human activity in a very large universe, the evil of greed and jealousy—all these are explored in the context of the "Star Trek" science fiction frame. The futuristic orientation suggests that these problems, more basic than the technological problems that allowed the new civilization to arise, will stand and be with us. Even in the face of improved social relations as expressed by the *Enterprise*'s mixed crew, humans must still face themselves and form groups. Standing in the way of successful societies in the future—and by direct implication, of our own— are evils which must be rooted out. In demonstrating the lasting nature of such problems the science fiction formula turns our observations on the present.

The importance of these shows as devices that allow a closer and more perceptive look at our contemporary world is increased by their structural difference from the other forms of television art we have examined. While the adventure shows are presented as self-contained episodes, they also create a sense of continuity, of relatedness, which makes their worlds less fantastic, for all their adventure, than the worlds of situation comedy or detective shows. It is true, obviously, that the action of any given episode in any of these series can be concluded. The problems are solved and the solutions depend on the same sense of heroism, of improbable capability, as they do in other shows.

Inherent in the adventure formula, however, is the fact that the central premise, the reason for the adventures to occur, cannot be concluded, ended, solved, in a single hour-long performance. The motivating problems must not be solved, or the series will cease to exist. Buzz and Todd cannot suddenly discover a meaningful life in some small town, on a farm, or in an office. Richard Kimball cannot be caught and he cannot cease to run. Either option would betray the series. When it did finally conclude after a number of successful years on the air, the producers chose to bring events to conclusion rather than remove the show without explanation. The motivating problem was solved, the one-armed man located, the detective satisfied, and Kimball allowed to rest. The starship *Enterprise* did suddenly cease to appear, but its audience has not allowed it to die. It runs in many areas in perpetual reruns, and an ever-expanding group of fans have formed associations, are publishing magazines on the subject and are even holding conventions.

What this suggests is that while the heroes can solve the problems that form the content of individual episodes, they are reminded by a number of factors that they are less than heroic. They have yet to solve the problems of their own lives, whether those problems be wanderlust, the threat of injustice and death, or the necessity to explore the reaches of space. The structure is that of the picaresque, a series of adventures within a larger framework. These shows approach a form that might be called novelistic. A larger world is tentatively created, in which the episodes appear. The sense of continuity brings the problems of those episodes closer to our own sense of probability. The shows do not go so far as to say that explicit problems are insoluble. Nor do they create a sense of memory, of history, that parallels our own. They merely tantalize the audience with the prospect of a more realistic sort of continuity. It remains for other shows to take the structure a step further and demonstrate that television can create a more complex fictional world.

7

SOAP OPERA: APPROACHING THE REAL WORLD

Rachel, the child of a broken home, has led a life deprived of normal childhood delights. Her mother, Ada, works hard and tries to instill the proper moral virtues, but Rachel emerges as selfish and spoiled. She sees a chance to climb socially by marrying Dr. Russ Matthews, son of a prominent Bay City family and a bit of a dullish character. After the marriage Rachel becomes bored with her life and engages in a brief affair with Steve Frame, young financier on the rise, and becomes pregnant. Steve is about to marry Alice, sister of Russ. Rachel walks into the engagement party and informs Alice that she is carrying Steve's baby.

Alice runs away to France to work in a hospital. Steve hates Rachel. Russ divorces her. She bears and keeps her son, Jamie, and moves in with mother Ada. Eventually Steve convinces Alice that his one mistake was just that, and they become the happily married young socialite couple. Rachel, too, seems to find happiness. She marries Ted, a typical loser, and for a time the two couples seem settled and occasionally even congenial toward one another. One source of continuing conflict is the child, whom Steve wishes to care for, whom Ted cannot support as richly. Suddenly we learn that Ted, who has opened a restaurant with money borrowed from Steve, has previously been involved with some small-time hoodlums who appear in Bay City and intimidate him in hopes of enlisting his aid in a narcotics deal.

Ted helps the police, but must go to prison for a year to pay for his previous actions. Rachel's long-lost father appears in town. Experienced in the nightclub business, he helps Rachel keep the restaurant open during Ted's absence. He also encourages her to see Steve, to get Steve to support Jamie, and ultimately to make an attempt to break up the marriage of Steve and Alice. The father arranges for Alice to walk in on Steve and Rachel during a conversation in which Rachel is declaring her love. Unknown to the two of them, Alice hears all and disappears to New York. Steve is once again distraught, but Rachel becomes more subtle in her approach. Each day she brings Jamie to see his father. Each day Steve must see Rachel. He is drawn to her and an affair begins.

Meanwhile, Alice has become the private nurse to the son of a wealthy New York executive whose wife is a shrew. The executive takes his son, and Alice, to St. Croix for a business holiday. The wife, assuming an affair is in progress, contacts Rachel, who then persuades Steve to take her to the island. There they encounter Alice. Steve does not understand the situation and refuses to believe the truth. They cannot reconcile their differences. Rachel divorces Ted. Alice divorces Steve. Steve and Rachel marry and, with Jamie, move into the house Steve built for Alice. Later, however, he learns of Rachel's manipulations and seems to be on the verge of yet another divorce in hopes of returning to Alice.

This sort of plot summary makes the soap opera the butt of so many jokes worn thin in the process of retelling. But the plot also indicates that soap opera breaks almost every rule of rigid framework and closely defined formula that we have established in previous discussions. The break with the larger patterns appears to move in two differing directions. On the one hand, there is an apparent negative quality in the production of soap opera. There is a loss of elegance with the daytime shows. They are not the polished, expensive productions that we see during prime time and to which we have become accustomed. This factor spills over into many other areas: into the creation of stereotyped plots such as the one recounted above, and into similarly extreme character types and methods of performance.

But these factors grow out of the essential difference between daytime serials and evening episodic television, the difference in time frame. Soap operas are not restricted to the sixty- or ninety-minute segment, and their insistence on letting stories grow and develop over periods of months and years brings them closer to experiential reality than any other form of video art. This use of time leads to a different use of events and actions, different modes of characterizations, and finally to a different set of values than that found in most of television. The result is that we get more indication of what television art can be through an analysis of soap opera than through examination of any other program type.

Doing so makes demands on us as audience. A recognition of the importance and power of this form depends on our willingness to relinquish some of our more commonly held aesthetic notions. It depends on a closer look at unexamined assumptions about the nature of popular art. What we must realize is that what we have seen in the past and judged as negative qualities are integral parts of a complex form; they are the qualities that define soap opera.

Nothing is more apparent in the world of soap opera than its essential physical flimsiness. Sets are noticeably thin; walls quiver when doors are shut too vigorously. The importance of this observation becomes obvious when we realize that there is almost no external world on daytime television. We know we are entering a hospital from the outside when the camera offers a close-up of the identifying plaque on the corner of the "building." When we must move from one town to another, we move in an automobile mock-up, usually without even the back-shot of filmed moving traffic. The automobile sounds are far more unrealistic than those of sophisticated radio programs. The lighting remains the same indoors or out. Rocks are cardboard; grass is plastic. Most importantly, no attempt is made to disguise these facts. We are always clearly in a television studio, on location in the world of soap opera.

Partially as a result of this sort of technicality, place is defined by function. A doctor's office is so designated by the "whiteness" of tables and pans, by diplomas on the walls, and by medical books on the shelves. There may be a memento on the desk which establishes a medical tone or which links the doctor to his family and the world outside his profession. In many ways the office is indistinguishable from that of the lawyer, which also displays books and diplomas. The lawyer's office is likely to be more clearly adaptable to use by clients. There are more chairs; there is a richer look of mahogany and leather rather than steel and plastic. The businessman can fit between these two categories. Depending on his degree of affluence and success, the office will be more like the lawyer's or the doctor's; the wealthier he is, the less functional his office. Restaurants consist of a few tables, a bar, a piano. A counter-cultural "coffee shop" will be dimly lit, with an unfinished floor, old tables, and posters covering the walls.

The set becomes an abstraction. There are clearly enough identifying features to establish a relationship with the world as most of us know it. We have been in a doctor's office and we know that this is, roughly, what one looks like. On the other hand, the set is symbolic, a functioning part of this carefully defined world. Similarly, certain types of things go on in doctors' offices; that is why so many doctors appear in the casts. In order to represent this type of activity, this type of character, the office becomes the link with that other world of the soaps.

This same sort of quality holds for the domestic interiors of the shows. As in the situation and domestic comedy much of the action of the daytime shows takes place in the homes of the characters. Most of these are solidly upper-middle class. Taste in furniture and design is traditional to modern. There are no ancient Victorian houses redecorated in starkly modern interiors. Things are soft and comfortable. There is usually a fireplace. Over it hangs a painting or a mirror, and around the room are small pieces reflecting the personality of the inhabitants. As subject matter begins to vary in a series, we may be admitted to the "pad" of a hippie or even the hovel-like room of the drug addict. Again, definition is minimal, representational, symbolic. It depends on the severest stereotype. What we are supposed to see is rooms defined by the people who live in them. Thus, the bachelor apartment is sometimes "created" by the fact that a bed is visible from the living room.

This pattern is so strongly a part of the soap opera form that even when some series open up to action in new, exotic locations, the abstractions remain the same. Recently characters have opened gift shops and small cafés. They have traveled to island resorts and have been on picnics or in jail. In every case the locale is represented rather than presented.

To a large extent these physical abstractions are dictated by the demands of budget and time. The shows are produced one or two days ahead of their air date. They are videotaped in small studios on sets that must be quickly shifted to represent a different type of location. But the factor has become so strongly a part of the shows that we can see the same sort of abstraction in another way, as it affects the people who appear in the dramas.

Almost exclusively these characters are the emblems of the upper-middle class. Professionally there is an overwhelming preponderance of doctors, lawyers, and businessmen. Women are generally well educated and often follow one of these same professions. When they choose to remain at home, they are cast as the stereotype of the upper-middle-class housewife, worried more about the problems of her children or about social affairs than about shopping or cleaning the house.

For the most part the people are elegantly but tastefully groomed. The men dress conservatively even when casual. The women are carefully trimmed in stylish fashions, coiffed in the most fitting styles. The appearance is carried into their homes, where that softness we have mentioned complements the appearances of persons.

In some cases, as in "Return to Peyton Place," the homes of the very rich point up the symbolic function of design most powerfully. Martin Peyton's mansion, now occupied by his grandson, Rodney Harrington, and his wife, Betty, is dripping with opulence. Colored marble columns rise to the painted ceilings. A curved staircase dominates a huge entryway. The study is paneled in the richest wood. The point here is that the audience must gauge its social responses to such clues. Any departure from the norm of upper-middle-class stability results in this sort of blatant representation in which richness is defined exclusively by material artifacts. Just as the rich are characterized by their extravagant homes, so is the addict's room defined by its squalor. Such images are presently entering the soap opera world, breaking a more traditional pattern of restricted class content. But they are presented in the most simple, the most obvious manner.

Equally simple are the traits of nonstandard characters. Their speeches must be filled with the clichéd versions of yesterday's slang. A hippie dresses from the files of news magazine stories of the 1960s rock scene. Poor farm wives appear as embarrassing sisters of wealthy businessmen, dressed in the classic mail-order "house frock." Their grammar is faulty and they often apologize for not being better educated.

The same process of stereotyping occurs with regard to race. As more and more black characters appear in soap operas, there emerges a highly self-conscious attempt to place them in roles that are identifiable to the audience. On the one hand, this means that they appear as nurses and bartenders. In another way they also appear in professional roles as successful young lawyers and doctors. Both types of role reflect an audience awareness of black cultural mobility. Some characters appear in the socially acceptable roles that have always been identified with blacks, whereas others demonstrate a permitted rise into white upper-middle-class society.

It is all a part of a "sign language" that the audience

recognizes and understands immediately. The visual aspects of the code, the technical representation of soap operas, are as easily translatable as the symbolic settings and social structures.

When these standardized characters in their stock professions enter the paper-thin world of studio representation, the cameras make no attempt to deceive the viewer into thinking that something more exciting is about to happen. In the soaps we are offered an almost unrelieved view of the faces of our characters. It is rare that more than three characters appear in a single shot, and in most cases we see only two characters. In these scenes it is also rare that we are offered more than a head-and-shoulders close-up. Only when a character is left alone, or is leaving other characters, do we become aware of his or her legs and full-length arms. Camera placement is obvious and the shifts indicate the use of only a few cameras.

All of this is possible because there is no real "action." Our concern is with dialogue, and the camera insists that our attention remain there, offering us a close-up of either the speaker or the listener. For variety we are given a close two-shot of both characters. Our eyes are restricted to the faces and facial expressions of full-screen magnitude. At times we have over-the-shoulder shots of one character reacting to another. In the most innovative shows we may be exposed to rooms filled with people, but even then we are quickly focused onto the speakers.

There is, then, no action in soap opera, nothing of the sort we are used to in prime-time programming. The simplest movements—sitting or standing, walking across rooms—often appear stilted. More violent motions appear as the height of contrivance. The fact that soaps frequently deal with violent content, with sexual encounter, murder, or physical involvement of one sort or another, does not alter the situation. This is a world of words.

Actors must learn not a methodology of body, but one of mind. Characters exist because they are "written," and the interpretation of character depends on an ability for introspection and reaction. Dialogue is all-important. Complex reactions on the part of characters must be communicated directly to the audience, hence the full face shots of characters who are obviously disturbed or satisfied or passionate. These shots often occur as a fade-out begins, cueing the audience to a whole set of emotional and psychological interactions. Because so much of the content depends on introspection, the soap operas have developed a usage of interior monologue more than any other type of television show. We are frequently engaged with voice over action sequences, with the visual representation of imagined events, or with memory. Often we see the creation of aberrant psychological states or dreams.

The excessive wordiness and restricted physical movement would seem to make soap opera the most static of forms. And indeed, this is the case if we use traditional categories for comparison. In place of the usual sorts of action, however, the soaps have created several other forms of movement which begin to demonstrate a unique sort of aesthetic preoccupation.

In the first place, keyed to the psychological focus of the shows, there is a movement provided by the music of the soaps. This is one of the most obvious and most often parodied of soap opera devices. In many cases the music is provided by the studio electric organ and is reminiscent of the days of radio soaps. It provides transition of time and place, offering an aural representation of the character's state of mind, predicting the doom or the joy that is to follow from a given incident. In some cases there has been a shift to full orchestra, or to some form of incidental music, but the effect is the same. From the opening theme to the closing dramatic chords, we know where we are because of the sounds.

There is also a type of lateral movement developed by an almost constant extension of subplots. While the focus of each show may remain with a small, identifiable group of people such as a family extended through marriage and close friendship, we will also be treated to the doings of other people who touch these central lives. We move widely through a community, entering house after house, watching similar reactions of some groups, the disparate actions of others.

Because these subplots do work themselves out in various ways, another type of movement is necessary. With the constant addition of new characters we are offered a type of vertical or extended movement. As the subplots grow and admit us to new subplots, we need new characters. Frequently they are the obvious creations of the growth of the script, necessary in order to find a sort of after-the-fact filler. At other times we are carefully prepared for their entry as a character indicates that he or she is about to be visited by the past. These types of movement, together with the constant introspection of all the characters, make up for any loss of physical action.

I should emphasize here that none of this is meant to imply negative criticism of the soap opera form. The elements defined above are the distinguishing elements of soap opera and they are marks of excellence within the form. They work. They are the features upon which are built the more serious structural elements of the soaps. They reinforce the technical reality of the world of soap opera. That type of reality has special features that we must define before we criticize.

As I have said, this technical reality thrives on a lack of actual representation. What is presented, however, appears to approach the specific world of the viewer fairly closely. The confined world of the housewife resembles the confined world of the television screen. People move about in rooms, in houses; they speak to one another in close contexts; there are no overhead or panoramic shots indicating a point of view other than that of the viewer. Indeed, there are no panoramas, no mountains, no prairies, no visions of skylines or shots of suburban sprawl. The viewer has been admitted to the lives of some other persons, and the old TV cliché "Thanks for letting us come into your living room" has been acted out.

The content of this world moves in this technical framework on a parallel plane. It, too, is a technical type of reality. Yet, at the same time, it approaches the world of the viewer in a realistic sense. Soap opera content is confined almost exclusively to a consideration of vitally human problems. But they are not dealt with as universals, as the old verities. Instead, they are focused upon and magnified to an overwhelmingly individual point. Consider the following plot summary capsulized from the now defunct "Bright Promise." The series began as a sort of academic soap opera. We were asked to interest ourselves in the interior goings-on of a small college town, and we focused on a number of families from the faculty and administration of the institution. For various reasons that aspect of the show disappeared quickly, and it limped along as a straight community-oriented show for another two years before folding. The plot summary comes from the academic phase.

Bill, a young English professor, a Romanticist, is caught in a perplexing situation. He is strongly attracted to one of his more responsive female students, Sandy, and she is attracted to him. They have convinced themselves that theirs is a totally innocent relationship, despite the fact that Bill is often forced to lie to his wife in order to cover for seeing Sandy. George, a coldhearted Medievalist, is jealous of Bill's professional success and of his success with Sandy. He decides to use his knowledge of the situation in order to "get" Bill by spreading his information throughout the community. He tries several times to force his own affections on Sandy by blackmailing her with his knowledge of her relationship with Bill. On one occasion he visits her apartment while she is out, and in an argument with her roommate, pushes the girl to the floor, where she strikes her head on a sharp object and dies. Having conveniently stolen Bill's library card earlier in the day, he leaves it with the body and Bill is soon charged with murder. In the course of the trial his involvement with Sandy is exposed and his wife leaves him. Through the efforts of his wife's brother, who serves as one of his lawyers, Bill is cleared. The truth is discovered and George, recently appointed chairman of the English Department, confesses to the "accident" on the witness stand.

Here, of course, we could argue that whatever interest there is in such a show resides in its topicality. There is growing interest in the goings-on of academic communities. But topicality is hardly ever a functioning device in soap opera. Though generational differences have always formed a part of standard complications in soaps, they have only recently been used in terms of counter-cultural conflict. As indicated, blacks are appearing more frequently, but the problems of militancy, indeed, even of integration, as a socially relevant issue are minimally dealt with. If one were unfamiliar with the form, it might be possible to argue that the interest in this show resides in a kind of sensationalism: extramarital relations, murder, murder trial. But the pattern is so common to soap opera that this could hardly be the case. The fact that this story, in the technical reality of soap opera, is so unsensational gives us the clue to its real importance.

Bill is simply a good man. All the rhetoric of the story indicates this. But he is a man who makes mistakes, and those mistakes are not to be rectified in the space of the half hour or hour allotted to the formulaic nighttime television show. His mistakes grow, they multiply and expand with his deception and with the maliciousness of his colleague until they almost consume him. As in "Bright Promise," most of the problems forming the center of soap opera plots can be defined best in the areas of physical or emotional pain. Good men go about their business, only to have it confounded by their scheming partners, their unfaithful wives, or some combination of both. Women who gave up their children for adoption after an adolescent "mistake" begin years later to search for them, intruding into the lives of those who took them in. Faithful mothers must face their daughers' unwanted pregnancies or painful divorces. The pattern of accidental death followed by trial for murder is repeated again and again.

This pattern of continuing and overwhelming human pain is defined and controlled by one of the most important aspects in the world of technical reality that comprises soap opera. There is no humor in that world. There is, on occasion, an interlude of peace of mind. There are quiet moments when families are assured of their ultimate love for one another; there are reunions and marriages and births; there are smiles. But there is never raucous laughter, pure delight, overwhelming joy, or even the mildest ribaldry. There are no comic characters, no contrived situations that can be built into comic structures. It is as if the world of situation comedy reruns in the morning precedes the world of soap opera afternoons. The hilarity of the one appears to match the drudgery of the other. Ultimately, however, the two worlds are not part of the same vision and will never meet. For while the situation comedy is doomed to repeat itself in every episode of every series, changing only in the actual "situation" that precipitates the action, the soap opera will grow and change. In this resides the single most important defining factor of soap opera, the factor that distinguishes it from other formulaic television and from most other forms of popular art. It is organic rather than formulaic and repetitive.

This organic quality is the result of several related factors. We see the same characters in soap opera week after week, just as we see the same characters on typical evening dramas. But the soap opera characters change. They grow older; they marry; they have children; their problems are always appropriate to their situation. The expanding subplots and lists of characters are open-ended. One character's problem leads to another's, or may necessitate the introduction of an altogether new character. If an actress leaves the series, she is replaced by another, and the character continues unless she is written out of the cast. Characters exist independently of the actors and actresses who portray them. In any case of change, some adjustment is necessary on the part of the audience. The situation, the surrounding characters, the "world" of the series, continues, however, even if the departed or changed character is central. Because of these factors, there is a strong degree of audience involvement which results in the possibility of writer and producer response to an audience reaction. Fan mail, rating reports, and any other available indexes of response to new characters or situations may result in changed characters or situations. The following events from the original nighttime version of "Peyton Place" indicate the sort of change that is possible.

When the show begins, young Rodney Harrington is something of a high school lover. It is clear that he is having his first serious affair with Betty Anderson, even though the first real complication of the show is his attraction to Allison McKenzie. As his feelings for Allison grow, we learn that Betty is pregnant with his child. In a violent reaction to this news Rodney wrecks his car and both he and Betty are injured. Betty loses the baby, but does not tell Rodney and he is forced to marry her. When it becomes apparent that she is no longer pregnant, and as our dislike for her deceptions increases, Rodney's father, who is having an affair with Betty's mother, arranges a divorce for the couple. Our attention is then centered for some time on the development of Rodney's affection for Allison. In the meantime, Betty matures, becomes a good friend of Rodney and Allison's, and after some time marries Stephen Cord, Rodney's archenemy and unknown half-brother. Stephen and Betty Anderson Harrington Cord become quite popular, their roles change to emphasize positive qualities, and they take a share of the central focus of the series. Mia Farrow, however, who plays Allison, decides to marry Frank

Sinatra, an event not recorded in the series, but very much a part of it, and must be written out of the show. For a time Rodney moves through a series of minor romantic attachments, but it is clear that his heart again belongs to Betty. Stephen Cord becomes a villain once again, and his jealousy drives Betty back to Rodney. When the show ended, we were primarily concerned with the relationship of Rodney Harrington and his new wife, Mrs. Harrington Cord Harrington. Unfortunately, Rodney was, at the time, paralyzed from the waist down and was having serious thoughts about his wife's relationship with her former husband. Later, the show was revived in a cheaper daytime version, "Return to Peyton Place." It still could not decide which of the two men deserved Betty, for though married to the now recuperated Rodney, she had just borne Stephen Cord's child when that series also folded.

The cancellation of the prime-time version of the show is doubtless attributable to a number of complex interactions. It was the first evening soap opera and was pitted against the popularity of several different shows at once, appearing as it did on two or three nights during the week. Doubtless, the audience was different, or was in a different mood from that of a daytime soap opera. The show depended heavily on a star system that played itself out. Too much attention was paid to personality and not enough to the characters as they existed in the story. I would also suggest that the show ended because it did not fulfill many of the categories defined above as essential elements in successful soap opera. Its primary similarity was to good TV drama with all its competent acting and technical excellence. Its subplots were like mini-dramas, working themselves out in well-resolved terms.

It should be apparent by now that the true soap opera differs in its value structure from all of the other forms of television art we have so far examined. The other forms depend on a star system that will not allow for a change in the central focus of a continuing series. These shows create the illusion of change through a shifting variety of situation, but we know from the beginning of each that the main characters, the hero figures, are never to be harmed or destroyed because they can never leave the show. We know in comedy that the characters will never change because any change would eliminate the comic premise on which the "situation" is created. In typical television fashion, the characters who appear in even the best of the prime-time series are frozen at the end of each episode without memory. They will appear next week as they appeared this week. The specific content will shift, but the formula and the formulaic responses will remain the same. In doing so they will reinforce those cultural patterns, cultural values, that we have established in previous analyses. The necessity for order, the power of the family, the dependence on authority, will all be presented in some fashion as we proceed into each episode.

This is not the case with soap opera. It is true that we have formulaic actions. As we have seen, the patterns of infidelity, or intrigue, of action bordering on incest, occur over and over. So, too, do certain character types. Each series has its stock roles: the heroic doctor, the "normal" sister, the stoic mother, the confidant, the conniving ingenue, the weak male, and so on. But the audience sees a different set of problems here than it sees presented at night, and these are far more closely related to the problems of the audience than the continual diet of spectacular murder solved by the spectacular detective. Consequently, these are the more "real" problems. They are unencumbered with imaginative leaps into the past for western adventure or into the pseudo-hip world of teen-aged police officers or into the strange remote world of ultra-glamorous publishers and reporters. The problems approached by soap operas are so close to those of its audience that it would seem to be uncomfortable. At times we must wonder how there can be such a massive audience for a world of almost unrelieved pain in which juvenile mistakes return to haunt the same characters when they become middle-aged mothers; in which success over one set of problems only seems to lead to new complications in a new subplot.

It is here, I would argue, that the true power of the form lies. For the world of the soap opera is more painful, more harsh, more unrelieved, than the world of the audience, and yet the characters always survive. The values are not those of overwhelming success in which right always conquers. They are those of pure survival, complicated by ambiguity and blurred with pain even in its most sought-after accomplishments. The values are not ambiguous in the false sense of the situation drama, in which right is sometimes painful in its success, for the characters in those dramas never remember the following week that they were faced with a dilemma a week before. And in situation comedy no father ever turns to his son and asks him to remember the lesson so beautifully taught a few weeks ago. By contrast the characters of soap opera must live for years with their mistakes and watch the implications multiply with each passing day.

Combining to perfect this presentation of values are all the elements described above. The actors do not overwhelm the audience with a sense of artistic flair. Instead, they respond and react in a manner suitable for the full-screen, direct confrontation. They grow old as their audience does, and their children turn on them in the same ways, refuse to learn or to accept advice. Even their bodies turn on them, and we see some actors and actresses of long standing grow fat and wrinkled. The technical facilities never come between the audience and the cast. The constantly developing complexity of subplots and the huge variety of personality approach more nearly a world like that of the audience. The reality of that world is indeed false in its lack of humor, of relief, in its imitation of everyday speech which sounds banal to the ear accustomed to nighttime drama. The characters' survival in spite of these deficiencies only serves to transfer some of the pain of the audience away from itself. Ultimately, in its pattern of growth and continuance, we are led again and again to the assertion that existence in itself is of great value and that survival is the measure of its worth.

Out of this rises a situation in which audience and show are inextricably linked, far more tightly than in most evening shows. The producers, of course, are quite aware of this link and use it to foster their form of daytime art. One result is a far more self-conscious move to explore more socially relevant issues. Agnes Eckhardt Nixon produces soap operas. In claiming that ours is the true golden age of TV, and in suggesting that the real worth of it is in the daytime programming she comments on the form's ability to become a factual part of viewers' lives:

. . . implicit in the serial is the opportunity to give an important subject an in-depth treatment, over weeks and months, which is impossible on any nighttime series that must have a new theme, or message, in each episode.

Thus, a five month campaign to inform women of the efficacy of the Pap smear test in detecting uterine cancer in its early stages brought a bonanza of mail from appreciative women across the country, many of whom, having followed our advice and discovered the condition in themselves, claimed we had saved their lives. [*Television Quarterly*, Winter 1972, pp. 51–52]

The same sorts of "real" problems have been explored in the realms of racial prejudice, venereal disease, drug addiction, and human sexuality. Always the result is the same. People respond to these televised versions of their own lives as they do not respond to the more flamboyant fictional presentations on prime-time television.

So real have soaps become for some people, and so unlike nighttime TV are they, that they have attracted the attention of some clinicians as possible therapeutic tools. They suggest for Dr. John R. Lion, a psychiatrist at the University of Maryland Medical School, a way to counter the problem of a fantasy world in which many people now seem to live.

In the end, I think the most realistic programs on TV are the soap operas. They portray life with all its complexities and insolubilities. Many of my patients are helped by watching them, and I often suggest to patients who have an overly glamorized view of the world that they view these programs in order to see, in admittedly caricatured form, what life is like. I suggest more soap opera, showing the lives say, of criminals and their inner torment. I suggest showing the inner workings of the mind of a wealthy executive, and I suggest that we are shown by the media how empty the life of the Godfather really is. [Baltimore *Sun*, February 18, 1973]

Ms. Nixon remarks on the same idea from the producer's viewpoint.

Protagonists with whom the viewers most identify today, the ones they champion most, often take the wrong step, make the wrong judgement and must suffer the consequences. They're human.

That suffering of the consequences is, this writer submits, key to a serial's popularity and longevity. For any dramatic entertainment to be a success in 1972 it must be relevant. And relevance repudiates the cliche of the sunset fadeout, of Nirvana on earth. In contemporary society, the mind viewing the small screen knows, if it knows anything, that life is not perfect, and that man has caused the imperfections. He caused them and must "suffer the consequences"—from a family quarrel to a global war. Thus a certain kinship is established between the fictional characters with their problems and the viewer at home with his. The viewer naturally wishes to see how these TV neighbors cope with their misfortunes, day by day, week in, week out, year after year. Audiences are bound, not by the chains of hero worship, but by the easily recognized bonds of human frailty and human valor. [Nixon, loc. cit.]

Human frailty and human valor are the province of all complex art. Much popular art ignores the specifics of this task, working instead with veiled and not-so-veiled cultural assumptions about ways in which human problems can be eliminated by heroic action, gentle advice, or slapstick resolutions. Soap operas have managed to deal with both aspects, with the entertainment function of the popular arts and with the crucial human functions of responses to problems. They stand between most of television and a number of new television productions that are reaching for a newer version of popular art.

These new shows break the ground for defining a television aesthetic common to this art form rather than an adaptation of other forms long established with their own forms of treatment. Before examining the newer versions, however, we are left with another task. We must realize that the formulas of television affect not only the content of their shows but the content of our lives as well. Crucial to understanding the power of television in the shaping of attitudes and perceptions is the manner in which "reality" is molded to fit our video expectations. We should now see how television creates entertainment out of the events of our lives.

8

NEWS, SPORTS, DOCUMENTARY: REALITY AS ENTERTAINMENT

So far we have been dealing with television's ability to use existing fictional forms and to create its own forms in the fulfilling of an entertainment function. By contrast television news is supposed to be "factual," and other forms such as sports, biography, and documentary are supposed to be "real" in a sense that other programs are not. Even television's severest critics are willing to praise these less "frivolous" features. To some degree most of us are willing to accept them as "pure information," or to put it more extremely, as the "truth." It is interesting to note in this context that studies have indicated that most audiences consider TV the most reliable of the news services, probably due to its visual component. But it should be clear by now that the relationship between fact and fiction, between reality and fantasy in the popular arts, is much more complex than the simple distinction would indicate. We know, for example, the "facts" of the historical West. We know that some of those facts are embodied in the mythical Western of popular construction. We also know that television restructures both of those sets of facts in the creation of its own form of the Western. Similarly, we have seen the creation of the documentary police series, and in an even more complicated situation we have seen television's doctors and lawyers offering us facts as part of their fictions, teaching us how to cure our sicknesses, spiritual, mental, physical, and social. Given such uses of reality, it should come as no surprise that television news coverage should also come under critical scrutiny which sees it as slanted or structured in particular ways to present particular viewpoints. The meanings of such restructurings, however, cannot be reduced simply to political motivation, to the preference of one set of facts over another. In order to understand the unreal quality of TV's "real" programs, one should not turn to the ideology of a particular set of writers or reporters, but to the fictional structures that news, sports, and documentary reflect.

Two recent essays have approached the problems of television from the standpoint of art and have reached similar conclusions: that the meaning of these shows is remarkably similar to that of television fiction as we have been defining it and that the function of character in structuring action is crucial. In "Art and Artifice in Network News," Dan Menaker argues for the following pattern of significance.

Each of the evening network news shows begins with a scenario. On CBS Walter Cronkite, often scribbling copy up to the last second, is first seen in profile. An announcer, speaking somewhat loudly over the exciting chatter of teletype machines, introduces the show and Cronkite; he then recites the name and location of each correspondent, as the same information is superimposed in white printing over the opening shot. On NBC John Chancellor sits to the side of an oversized calendar month, with today's date circled, and tells the audience about the stories to be covered, often suggesting interrelationships among them. On ABC the opening format is a bit more complicated, but Reasoner and Smith do make use of pictures for the lead stories and a listing for the less important ones.

> On each network the ritual opening establishes the theme of the entire program: excitement governed by order. [*Harper's*, October 1972, p. 41]

Presiding over this creation of order, says Menaker, are the anchor men who perform as "consummate actors, even if they are simply being themselves." Cronkite is possessed of a "paternal persona" which "has been the subject of much analysis." Roger Mudd "sounds and looks substantial." John Chancellor is "less the father and more the friend—the friend who knows a lot and lets you in on it." Reasoner is "open and vulnerable—an innocent, impressionable man-child. His colleague, Howard K. Smith, "is prudent and authoritarian, though his high voice offsets the firmness a little." David Brinkley is "smart-alecky, cynical, impish," while Eric Sevareid "represents pure reason besieged by irrational extremism."

Most of the players in the three troupes are physically attractive and aurally elegant. An obese, ugly, or squeaky-voiced newsman, though he might be professionally qualified, could not meet the non-journalistic requirements of a network correspondent's job. The competition for ratings, one assumes, must lead the three organizations to seek reporters with stage appeal, which, like dramatic structure and entertaining graphics, to some degree blurs the audience's vision of reality. [Ibid., p. 47]

The point of Menaker's analysis is that we don't have far to go to find the prototypes for these figures. They exist in the realm of popular television, and the tasks they perform are directly related to those performed by similar star-heroes of the programs that precede and follow their presentation of the news. In a penetrating examination of this mix Curtis McCray outlines the blend of fantasy and reality, of advertisement and program, of juvenile television and hard, real news. At the heart of his study is a comparison of Cronkite and Captain Kangaroo. Both men, he suggests, are guides, both mentors. More importantly, they both assume a fictional identity that transcends mere reality.

Captain and Walter are the title characters and heroes of their shows. As surely as Ben Cartwright will make the decisions, moral and metaphysical, of which we approve, so we know they will not disappoint us. Or, perhaps a better comparison is with the narrator in a novel like *Tom Jones*. That voice tells us where we are, supplies us with the moral norms with which to judge Tom, and reassures us that Tom will succeed despite desperate odds. Through the ups and downs of Captain's day, we never doubt that he will make it. In fact, we may enjoy his dilemmas more because we know that he will succeed. Through the ups and downs of the world's day, as Walter reports them, we never doubt that the world will make it. (Walter has been with us a long time. Who forgets his urging of Alan Shepard's Mercury flight—"Go, baby, go"—or his reporting of the deaths of JFK and RFK.) Walter is there, as he has always been, presenting, refining, informing, narrating, and hence reassuring us that regardless of how bad the content of the news may seem, the form of the show guarantees that he will be back tomorrow and the next day and the next. Captain lifts his phone to call Greenjeans at the barn when he needs something fixed. Walter calls to his men in the field and seems to us on the other side of the camera to have at his disposal the command of both infinite knowledge and power: Sydney, Hong Kong, Berlin; he roams the world

at will. Captain and Walter are heroes, centers of
their shows. Indeed, they may be the shows. I can
no more separate Walter from *Walter Cronkite and
the CBS Evening News* than I can separate Richard
Burton from *Hamlet* or Laurence Olivier from
Othello, or Richard Boone from the character of
Paladin. ["Kaptain Kronkite: The Myth of the Eternal
Frame," unpublished paper presented at the Popular
Culture Association Convention, East Lansing,
Michigan, April 1971, pp. 17–18]

McCray and Menaker also suggest that the implications of recognizing such an artistic structure go far
beyond the effect of restructuring information. "Is
Walter Cronkite real? I don't know," says McCray.

Probably not. At least no more real than Homer's
Odyssey, Virgil's *Aeneid,* or Dante's *Divine Comedy.*
But reality may not be a valid test of the goodness
of a TV show anyway. While I would make no
claims for the ultimate artistic greatness of *Walter
Cronkite* or *Captain Kangaroo,* I would argue that
formally the shows do tap us somewhere deeply in
the recesses of our culture's consciousness. [Ibid.,
p. 18]

Menaker puts it a bit more critically.

The three network-news programs are for many
Americans the only available mirror of the world at
large. And they are fun-house mirrors; they shrink,
elongate, widen, narrow, lighten, or exaggerate what
stands before them. I do not know whether these
images could be corrected or even that they ought
to be corrected. I do know that we must see them
for what they are, for we do not live in a fun house.
[Menaker, p. 47]

When such observations are placed within the total
television context being developed here we see the

increasing complexity of the aesthetics of television. It is true, obviously, that news programs take on artistic or perhaps even fictional frames. As indicated in the last chapter, however, it is also clear that fictional shows have begun to take on "factual" or "informational" frames. Shortly after McCray's paper was presented, for example, Walter Cronkite was guest for an entire week on Captain Kangaroo's program.

As in other forms of television entertainment the character who stands at the center becomes the defining factor. At the most mundane level this character is supposed to be a reporter, an intermediary, a transmitter of information. In doing so he must be actively involved, getting behind the scenes, locating the sources of action, discovering the centers of power. He must know how to talk to persons involved, the agents and reactors to events that have taken place. More than anything else he or she is expected to deal with human beings, and even when surveying the effects of a natural disaster or analyzing recent economic trends, the focus must be on the people who are involved. All of this begins to imply a process of selection and manipulation, for the news reporter is forced to shape materials according to the limits of time and space and facilities. In most cases news presentations are written and the whole question of literary style enters as another potent shaping factor. The result is that we refer to news "stories," and the term indicates our expectations of the same sort of structuring devices that we find in fiction.

This is one of the factors that lead to the observations of McCray and Menaker regarding the newscaster, particularly the news anchor person, as a sort of fictional character. Such a role is created by the fictional frame of the news show and by the total television matrix. Here, as the critics have observed, the central figure, like most television heroes, is not Odysseus or Galahad, but Father. Around him it is possible to identify all sorts of brothers and sisters, uncles and children. Since the news is able to give us excitement along with domestic drama, however, the more exciting characters are the younger sons and daughters of the stationary figure who sits in the studio and guides us through the maze of daily events. These young men and women are on the move, with the action. They appear everywhere, even though some of them may hold down traditional assignments from time to time. The excitement of their lives is expressed not only by the exotic nature of their travels but by the importance of their work as well. They keep us informed, and to do so, they must appear in all the centers of action; by definition they are close to the centers of power while we are not. Things happen around them as they happen around the heroes of spy and detective fiction; or at least, that is the way we perceive it.

Indeed, it is only a short step from the image of these real reporters to the image of the reporter in fiction. We are all familiar with the tough, cynical, crusading reporter of the newsroom. He is as exciting as any of the characters about whom he writes, and it is no wonder that "Front Page" and "The Big Story" were early television hits. As yet there has been no series involving a television reporter, but with "The Name of the Game" we were introduced to the glamour world of big-time magazines through the roles of reporters and publishers. Even the "girl Friday" assistant types in this series were directly involved in action and intrigue and visited exotic worlds dressed in the most up-to-date fashions while the men were being beaten and shot at. All of these shows were essentially mysteries, and the idea of the reporter as detective is one of the more potent aspects of the character.

As a result of these factors, the newsman becomes news, a star, an object of examination, of admiration, a public figure. In doing so he is forced to live his private life in a public fashion, and his role in one influences his role in the other. Like John Wayne or Jane Fonda, we expect reporters to show consistency between the two roles. When political figures build their lineups of stars and celebrities, we mentally calculate which of the news people will fall into the various camps. Sometimes we even know which associations are made because we discover the relationships from other informal sources.

Is it any wonder, then, that when we observe Ron Nessin dodging bullets in Vietnam or Cyprus or any one of a hundred other trouble spots, we begin to form an association in our mind with the reporters who behave in similar ways on television's fictional shows. Garrick Utley chooses to dress in 1940s styles, including the classic trench coat of the World War II reporter. When we see him exposing what appears to be yet another political scandal, can we distinguish him from the reporters and detectives who prowl about office buildings at night, breaking all the rules of propriety in order to conform to the rules of excitement and entertainment? If we see Sander Vanocur weeping unshamedly at the death of Robert Kennedy as he reports the event on television, can we forget that the two men were personal friends and that the reporter and many of his colleagues were often guests in the Kennedy home? These confusions become particularly important when we feel that a reporter's own political views are creeping into his or her broadcasts.

If we could not see these people, perhaps it would not be such an issue. Between the newspaper report- ers and their audiences there is a vast separation caused by print and by the structure of the form. Though radio brings the news somewhat closer, one must still listen carefully for tones and inflections that create personal involvement. With television it all comes together. The reporter writes the copy, and its style reflects certain directions taken. We hear the voice, modulated with ironic overtones, questioning, probing, suggesting interpretation. Most importantly, we see the reporter perform, and all the factors inter- weave a special sort of persona. It is possible for the reporter to editorialize with a slight smile, a nod of the head, a raised eyebrow, or a sinister overtone. Re- peatedly the audience is left with the impression that the newscaster questions what he must report as fact, or reports as fact that which he should question pri- vately. The result, naturally enough, is the editorial by-line in which the reporter clearly distinguishes be- tween observed "fact" and his opinion regarding the fact. But we are looking at people, not at lines of print, and people carry their own by-lines, become opinionators because they live in the multiple worlds we have described. Who can separate David Brink- ley's long career as a reporter and a friend of political liberals from his carefully insulated "Journal"? We listen to him now as we did when he was "merely" a reporter, and many people think that he is telling the "truth." Or who can make the leap that distinguishes Howard K. Smith's conservative editorials from his "objective" reporting? Every attempt to create mini-frames with which to isolate the opinions of reporters is overpowered by the frame already existing within the mind of the audience.

This same sort of transforming power is turned by television onto the American sports world. Sports, as games involving human beings, embody almost every aspect of popular entertainment. The idea of conflict is central. Legitimate violence is present in varying degrees in all athletic contests. Ultimately the sporting event as game focuses on the aspect of problem-solving, that pattern we have seen in all the entertaining forms of the popular arts. But unlike the socially oriented problems that form the content of most television programming, the sports game is much more like combat. Instead of value conflicts, generational differences, and human interaction, we have the basic tests of skill and strength. To maneuver the team down the field without losing the ball, to control play so that the opposing team achieves no runs for its hits, to loop the ball into the basket as the last buzzer sounds—these are the conflicts that have thrilled vast numbers of fans in the most traditional ways and that thrill millions more on television.

Sport has never served as mere entertainment in American culture. From Little League through high school, sports activities have been cited as a means of self-identification for participants. For parents, supporters, cheerleaders, and bands, sports frequently serve as the center for community activity. These identifications expand into the local semipro teams and the regional professional organizations, and the whole structure of classes, regions, and leagues serves as a cultural framework. For a young male, growing up in New York meant for many years a symbiotic relationship with one of the three major baseball teams located there. The Yankees, the Giants and the Dodgers took on symbolic, mythic proportions, and around the teams was built the whole mystique of gathering autographs, monitoring averages, and predicting success at the league or the "world" level. For millions of other fans far away from such centers of pure worship the teams were venerated via newspapers and radio, but always with the knowledge that the "home team" was a surrogate, embodying an ideal expressed far away in the elegant temples of competition. The idea that two American baseball teams were competing each year for the "world" championship title was a unifying concept. Sports offered cohesion and identity, the mythic model.

Because of the powerful visibility of the components of such a model, it has always been used as far more than either entertainment or cultural unifier. It is quickly transformed into a vehicle for cultural values, and we translate the playing field into an image for "real life." The virtues of practice, hard work, dedication, desire, competitive spirit, fair play, "good sportsmanship," and a host of other commodities are pointed out to generation after generation of young people. The language of the games, the initiations into rituals, the formalities of winning, are transformed into mystical moments. Sport is hallowed as holy text.

On the individual level all these virtues are located in the person and spirit of the sports hero. At the functional level he is simply a player who performs certain actions better than his colleagues and opponents, and is very much like the newscaster as conveyor of information. Because of his skill, however, he, too, becomes quickly translated into metaphor. Having accepted all the values associated with sport, and having practiced them with the rigor of any devotee, he attests to their truth. So we point to the lives of Lou Gehrig, Babe Ruth, Mickey Mantle, George Halas, Bart Starr, or John Unitas and scores of other heroes as examples of what is possible in America. If the hero has overcome a physical handicap in order to reach his position, or if he plays only at the cost of great physical pain, then the process of sports becomes a metaphor for healing. If he has risen from economic hardship, the sport becomes the route for social mobility. If he represents an ethnic group that is generally oppressed, then sports make obvious the equality of all Americans. If he becomes a millionaire, then sport is seen as a royal road to material success. So we translate the biographies of the heroes into children's books, into movies and television specials for adults. We are entertained by the narrative of their lives. We record the words they leave with us upon retirement as definitions of what it is to be American, and their humility on such occasions is marked down as another positive character trait.

The parallels between such games and their heroes and the structures and heroes of television are clear. Those fictional shows demonstrate the ability to solve problems by working within a defined set of values. A highly similar set of values is traditionally associated with sports, and those who practice them win. The sports heroes, then, are very conscious of their role as public figure and have generally behaved in a way that corresponds to the actions of our fictional models. When they have visited hospitals filled with handicapped children, they have done so consciously, as representatives of virtuous kindness. It is not so much that they teach us these values in the same manner as the fictional fathers, but that they stand as models of those who have been taught. The traditional image of the athlete as somewhat less than bright works here, and we see the sports hero accepting, without question, the obvious wisdom of the culture.

The pervasive power of television has changed much of this traditional function for sports and sports heroes. With television the regional or local identity of teams is destroyed. The man sitting in Arlington, Texas, can watch and enjoy the successes of the Los Angeles Dodgers with the same degree of interest as the man sitting in Brooklyn. When Arlington becomes the home of the former Washington Senators, the fan in Washington has the same opportunity. In any case it is likely that none of them can experience the degree of ecstasy once possible in Ebbets Field. The talk of sports is filled with strange names, and there is something bizarre about the massive football machine from tiny Green Bay, Wisconsin, mashing into submission its opponents from Chicago or Philadelphia. Collegiate sports become the supply centers for the professional camps, become professionally oriented in their own activities. School spirit remains, but as an adjunct to the competition for the number one position in the national polls, and the players on these teams are rated in terms of professional draft choices rather than as campus heroes.

The mystique of sport is gone, and as the pervasive eye of television turns onto the private lives of the players, the mystique of the sports hero goes, too. What are we to make of news items about our sports figures that do not appear on the sports page or in the sports segment of the evening news? Caught in such a media cross fire, fans and players alike are unable to respond consistently. The sports figure becomes a superstar, and as such may be unwilling to sacrifice his private life for the traditional image imbedded in the culture, defined by an almost fictional regard for the heroic position. The fans, on the other hand, are unwilling to see their heroes as anything less than mythic. The resulting conflicts create new attitudes toward sports and sports figures.

What sort of taboo is violated when baseball players actually resort to a strike in order to get more money, better benefits? Something very deep is touched as we watch fans turn against the players to side with the powerful big-business operation of the management. Perhaps it is simply a feeling that the players are all rich enough. Or perhaps it indicates that we do not wish to admit that these players, these "characters," in the drama of sport have real and apparently self-serving needs. If this is the case, how are we to deal with a Joe Namath or a Muhammad Ali?

On the one hand, we recognize Namath's marvelous physical ability. We even admit that because of physical ailments he generally performs under great stress and at personal sacrifice. At the same time, we have been made aware of his private life by those same agents that make us aware of his prowess. We are simultaneously intrigued and repelled by his image as swinging bachelor with the long hair, the penthouse apartment, the bevy of girls. Even if we can accept such individuality, we do not know how to react when we discover that Joe is co-proprietor of a nightclub financed by gambling interests. We would like to defend him, for many reasons, but we can't be sure. After all, he doesn't fit the image. Even more confusion is caused by his willingness to trade on his "Broadway" image to become a movie star, to make television commercials depicting him as swinger rather than as athlete, and to host his own television talk show.

Ultimately Namath is safe because all of his ventures stem essentially from his success, and once he is cleared of any criminal implication they do not threaten the basic values associated with American sport. Not so with Muhammad Ali, who is willing to allow his image to be defined in the realms of politics, religion, and race as well as in the more glamorous aspects of sports stardom. The myth of sports holds that it is an area of great freedom, without respect to racial distinction. Ali exemplified the myth on the one hand and flaunted it on the other. In developing the persona of the glib-mouthed poet who consistently refused to praise the abilities of his opponents, he offended the believers of the myth and began a movement that has demonstrated that black athletes are often used as gladiators in the camp of the majority, their services bought and sold without thought for the person. When Ali added to this character the already suspect trappings of the Black Muslim movement and consequently refused military service on religious grounds, he was flayed by the press and rejected by a previously awed public. The mythic values of sport had begun to clash with the new medium that brought sports into such enjoyable proximity to the American public. When viewers could actually see black athletes in the 1968 Olympics standing with clenched fists and bowed heads during the playing of the national anthem, many were outraged. It was the sight as much as the idea, and the knowledge that millions of viewers were seeing the same act was annoying and frightening. It was a bad image.

It was not bad because of its social criticism or because it reflected an individual choice. It was bad because it was not in the script, it violated our expectations. The result is a clash of symbolic gestures. The athlete as symbol of accepted values cannot also be the symbol of revolution—especially not in the televised version of the event.

There is a structure imposed on the raw event of sports activity, part of which is inherent in the idea of contest. Much more comes, however, from television's insistence on creating the dramatic frame within which the event occurs. As a result, the role of the sports announcer, many of whom are former sports stars, takes on increasing importance. The audience is told what to see and is told what it has just seen. Each movement and series of actions is interpreted by the announcers and commentators. Even before the games we are told what to look for. We are shown historical sequences in which the teams demonstrated, in past games, their techniques and specialities. After the game we are treated to analysis of what has happened, usually in the larger context of what the event will mean in the larger structure of competition for postseason prizes, bowls, ratings, series, and so on.

Central to this process is the role of the television director. He must decide what we actually see, and the cameras move skillfully to capture for us the moments and movements of greatest importance. It is here that the developing technology of television has played its largest part, with the invention and perfection of instant replay. Now we can see a single moment over and over; the commentators can refine their remarks accordingly. We can see in split screen and slow motion more of the action than we thought possible only a few years before, and we become increasingly sophisticated in our understanding of the skills involved in sports. As this happens, the narrative structures become more and more important. Now, in the new super stadiums being built in many large cities, huge television screens are being designed as part of the necessary equipment. The fans who attend the games will be treated to the same comforts of perception available to the home audience. Action and instant replay are telecast to the fans in the seats by closed circuit. This is not because they cannot see the live action on the field or court before them. Rather it is provided so that they can see it in certain ways and see it again. During time-outs and half-time breaks the fans are offered commercials for the arena's own facilities and for upcoming events. The screens also provide cartoon and film "entertainment," fireworks and waving flags during the playing of the national anthem, and they explode into riotous color when the home team scores. Such comforts have to do with the elements of narrative and frame, and though part of this structure comes from the games themselves, more of it comes from our knowledge of the television version of those games. That is the version that includes advertisement, directed viewing of events, and the technological advantages of repeated viewing of action.

Having become accustomed to the imposed structures that come to news and sports from more traditional areas of entertainment, we are willing to accept the restructuring of most events that occur in our own "real" world. Perhaps, in some cases, we depend on the structure to make sense of those things. This is most probably the case with our response to the national space program.

In a moment of high drama on television, President Kennedy suggested that America could place men on the moon in the decade of the 1960s, and partially in response to this call it was done. Seen by many as acts of surrogate war (the ultimate sporting event?), televised space activities were seen by most of the audience as "real" excitement, complete with the creation of new national heroes and new national myths. The structures of story and narrative were imposed from the start, and when it was over with the voyage of *Apollo* 17, one newscaster made a personal comment. Nostalgic and a bit saddened by the end, he suggested that it had been the excitement of the event as much as anything else that made it important for Americans.

We had seen it all before, of course, in the world of science fiction created for us in literature, movies, radio, and television. All these images existed in our minds, and when the astronauts looked so much like the first voyagers from the days of "Flash Gordon," the commentators had a field day pointing out the perceptive powers of those early creators of fantasy. As we waited for the reports to come to us across the reaches of space, as we thrilled during moments of impending crisis and failure, we could just as easily have been reading a novel by Jules Verne or Robert Heinlein. In fantastic mixes of "reality" we could watch news reports on the development of programs once part of the New Frontier, we could then see an episode of "Star Trek" which opened by telling us that space is the final frontier, and finally we could see a live telecast from inside a spaceship.

Aware of their role as superstars, the astronauts responded accordingly. They attempted to inject a bit of personality into the somewhat sterile world of the space program by sneaking corned beef sandwiches aboard the spacecraft to supplement their diet of pre-packaged foods. They carried golf clubs to the moon with which to make chip shots into craters. Some groups were much more conscious of the role of the artist than others, and staged live shows for the home viewers. The meager attempts at structure and form, the hand-lettered cards announcing the sequence of "acts," came across to the late-night viewer as a poor version of a home movie, or as an amateurish attempt to mimic a television variety show. The unshaven moon travelers, floating about their cramped space, seemed like versions of someone's ham of an uncle, clowning away the real importance of the event. At the same time such actions made the whole process more human, and when seen in the context of the drama imposed by the medium itself, it all fit together.

Given such raw material, it is no wonder that television turns its capabilities to making such events more dramatic. Soon the reporting takes on a heavy narrative tone, the missions are given poetic names, the astronauts are given the full biographical treatment, and the "missions" become even more like fiction. What is the audience to think, for instance, when it views a computer-perfected simulation of the exact movements of the men on the moon? Even when the astronauts are out of the range of their own cameras, these "realistic" representations show us what they are doing at the exact moment when they are doing it. Such devices might seem to be purely informative, but television cannot remain at that level. As a result, we see the activities not from the single angle of the astronauts' own camera, but are treated instead to shots worthy of the most artistic cinematographer. We watch enthralled as the camera rises from behind a pile of moon rocks to frame for us the departure of the spacemen riding away in their lunar vehicle, or as they happen upon a pile of interesting geological samples. All the while there at the bottom of the screen is the discreet notation in computer printout type, SIMULATION. But the simulations are so much more interesting than the live shots. With reality we're back to home movies again and nobody wants Uncle Harry when Flash Gordon is available. We immediately recognize familiar points of view. The shot from behind the rocks is usually the one that informs the audience that the spacemen are being watched by unknown eyes, may be in some sort of danger. It is the point of view that exists within our own television memory, and we sometimes wonder if the moments of drama and tension that occur within this world of near perfection are not structured for us in order to create excitement. Indeed, as the series of moon voyages progressed, the coverage and the audience seemed to grow weary of the repetition. There were no monsters on the moon, it turned out, and space was as bland as baseball without the series. football without the Superbowl.

This brings the problem full circle, back to the points made by Menaker and McCray. Television news and sports purport to show us reality when in effect the structures imposed by the medium and by the formulaic aspect of coverage closely approach those of the most fictional of television forms. The instant replay technology is developed for us in sports events, and as a consequence we see runner cross finish line, ball touch fingertips, glove meet flesh over and over again in immediate repetition. We view the same event from various perspectives. We know, though the referee may not, that a player stepped out of bounds while running for a crucial touchdown. The score counts just the same. Is the game, then, "real" or "fictional"? The same device is used in reporting other events. At 12:01 A.M. of New Year's Day 1973 we see an instant replay of 12:00, the moment of change. Which is real?

In an awesome, awkward moment in the early technology we see the jerky replay of Jack Ruby's arm rising, the grimace and collapse of the murdered Oswald. Again and again the newscasters play it for us until we anticipate each flicker. Was there any reality in such an event other than that imposed by the newscasters? We see film clips of Martin Luther King standing on the balcony of a Memphis motel moments before he is killed there. Then the camera shows us the same balcony through the window from which the shots were presumably fired. The audience now has the murderer's perspective. Similarly, another audience has the immediate perspective of those who followed Robert Kennedy into the kitchen of a Los Angeles hotel, heard the pop-gun sounds and screams, and saw another assassination victim lying on a bloody floor.

In Chicago at the 1968 Democratic Convention the television news did what it has always done, carrying us along in the structures of adventure, depending on the irony created by cutting from street riots to convention speeches. As the camera caught for us the bloody heads, the beleaguered policemen, the billows of tear gas, the moral outrage of the impeccably dressed Senator Ribicoff, and the moral indignation of Mayor Richard Daley, we repeatedly fell back to the device that stood between the audience and the action, to the calming voices of the announcers. When we began to see that the announcers, too, were directly involved, when their voices lost their calm, the involvement became too direct. The reactions to the coverage of the Chicago riots charged the television reporting with undue political editorializing, with one-sided attempts to explain the situation at the expense of the Chicago police. The medium was charged with offering its audience a "fictionalized" version of what "really" happened.

Clearly, the Chicago reporting had implications that extended beyond the realm of the transfer of information. But so does all reporting. It is only when the extensions offend certain people that the strong reper-cussions occur. When the case seems more neutral, we are willing to accept restructuring as appropriately stylistic. The same is true with the coverage of sports. So long as we feel that the view from the armchair is superior to that from the bleachers we leave the struc-turing of the game to the television director and a crew of commentator-interpreters. This was the case with the 1972 Olympic Games televised from Munich, Germany.

The Olympics have always been seen as show, as spectacle, and the Twentieth Olympiad was to be the greatest ever. Coverage was given to ABC, noted among fans and critics as the best sports network. The audience was promised and given a seemingly endless array of events from which to choose. We were taken behind the scenes to see the rigor of the training the athletes were required to undergo. We saw the depth of their dedication. In interviews with their families we saw the homes from which they came, walls and shelves covered with trophies that seemed to explain some of their motivation.

The extensive coverage began to pay off with an inordinate amount of drama. From the first the human conflict inherent in the competition was intense. The audience discovered an unexpected heroine in "little Olga Korbut" from the Soviet Union. We watched her brilliant performance on the uneven parallel bars one night, saw her fail there the next, and cheered as she returned to take a silver and two gold medals in her final individual events. With mixed feelings we listened to the confident attitude of Mark Spitz as he predicted a record number of victories for himself. Then we watched as his predictions came true.

Simultaneously we found ourselves directly involved in political turmoil of a kind that has plagued the Olympics during recent years. Charges and countercharges of professionalism were outweighed only by similar charges against the judging procedure. The ABC announcers were quick to point out that the East German diving judge was partial to Communist-bloc country participants and consistently put up lower scores for their opponents. Both fans in the arena and announcers were unable to follow the judging of the boxing competition. They jeered the decisions of the judges and watched in amazement as those same judges favored other fighters in apparent attempts to rectify their former errors. On the track racial tension flared again as it had four years previously. Two black American sprinters, having secured first and second places in their race, stood casually and conversed during the playing of the national anthem. They were immediately barred from further competition.

Suddenly all such incidents seemed trivial as we were informed that seven Israeli athletes were being held hostage by a group of terrorists representing an Arab nationalist organization. Initially such news was almost incomprehensible. Then we slipped into the news-as-drama formula, and the sports announcers became our reporter-guides. All day we watched via fixed cameras as the terrorists sent out notes listing their demands. We became familiar with the few perspectives of the building in which they had locked themselves. Other cameras, less restricted, recorded the arrival of vans of policemen and watched as they changed into athletic garb in order to be less conspicuous. The tension mounted as they climbed by circuitous routes to the tops of buildings and stood there with automatic weapons cradled in their arms. But no charge came, and by nightfall the kidnappers and their hostages had moved to the Munich airport, presumably in order to fly out of the country.

Finally, late that night two ABC announcers, Jim McKay and Chris Shenkle, sat in a barren studio waiting to give the audience final word of the action. There were reports of gunfire at the airport, and though the worst was feared, no official notification had come. McKay and Shenkle were forced to ad-lib for over an hour, repeating the series of events that had led to the moment. Peter Jennings, ABC's Mid-East specialist, in Munich on vacation, came to the studio to give political analysis and "background" information. Lou Cioffi, director of the news team that had covered the airport, came in to wait the official announcement, though there was every suspicion that he knew what was to be said. The waiting correspondents almost disintegrated into absurdity when they began to joke awkwardly about Jennings' Canadian accent. The news did come, and as feared, all the athletes and several of their captors had been killed in a combination of ill-timed and futile events at the airport.

At this point the capabilities of television came into

play and offered us a structure to which we could relate. Clearly, the situation in the studio was being stretched within the constraints of a timed, TV hour situation. At a crucial moment when no one seemed to have anything else to say, Shenkle turned to McKay and requested a "two-minute wrap-up" of the day's events. McKay agreed. The camera shifted away from the other three men and moved to a close-up of Mc-Kay's tense face. He started to speak in that tone so familiar to the viewer of television news, the measured cadences, the proper sentence structures, the concerned demeanor. "It began almost twelve hours ago with a knock at the door of the apartment . . ." and the perfect two-minute wrap-up followed.

This is not to suggest that McKay's comments, or his ability to formulate them, indicate insincerity. On the contrary, the emotional drain of the day showed clearly, and if anything, the wrap-up was beyond ordinary service. It does suggest, however, that the structures of television are so tightly built in that they are used, by the performers and by the audience, as a means of ordering the seemingly chaotic world that whirls around us. Thus, the memorial service for the murdered athletes was held on the next day and resembled, in more solemn fashion, the opening ceremonies of the games. And on the second day following, the games were reopened. The decision to continue the games reflected, according to the officials, a refusal to be intimidated by acts of violence. It also reflected a return to normalcy, and the conclusion of the Twentieth Olympiad seemed to reflect an attitude toward the competition that made it similar to the opening day. The killings had become the most important of a series of news stories to emerge from the days of sport. So long, then, as we remain in the world of the news show we are safe, and as other critics have indicated, the role of the newscaster is closely allied to that of the star in our fictional frameworks. The problem remains that these many worlds, the multiple worlds of television news and television fiction, of television fiction and our own worlds of experience, have become mixed, confused, and warped in strange ways.

A significant event in unfolding this intermingling of media and experience came throughout the spring and summer of 1973 with the telecasting of the hearings of the Senate Select Committee on Watergate. The hearings themselves were described from the beginning in terms of entertainment. The committee chairman, Sam Ervin, behaved as a consummate performer and could be compared with Marcus Welby or Billy Jim Hawkins in his willingness to lecture, to advise his witnesses. His mixture of rural and ancient wisdom linked him with any number of television characters who have assumed that the world would be simpler if people simply behaved themselves.

Other members of the committee found themselves thrust into a media spotlight and began to react accordingly. Some of them dressed differently. Others seemed to have a newfound importance, especially when their names were mentioned in the news by reporters telling the audience that the members had discovered a newfound importance.

The most telling aspects of the hearings came as the bizarre events connected with this political scandal began to unravel. There were spies and amateur spies. There were policemen and former policemen. There were payoffs and alleged payoffs. All of it smacked of a television adventure show. The code names and secret lists of enemies, the investigations and bur-

glaries, did not indicate that the audience was per-
ceiving the world in terms of television. Rather, the
strongest indication was that people in places of power
operated as a result of such a perception. While much
was made of the role of the press in uncovering the
events of Watergate—investigative reporting worthy
of a television series—the influence of the media on
high-ranking officials was the most obvious disclosure.
People care about their image, about the image of
their enemies, about the attitude of the newscasters,
and on through a list of television-related subjects. It
was as if behavior were determined by many of the
same structures we have been examining. The upshot
was the discovery of such behavior and the immediate
recognition that here was a set of problems that
would not be solved within the single hour's format.
There were no heroes capable of overcoming the complications of the scandal.

Watergate, then, provides an ambiguous situation
that remains (at the time of this writing) unsolved,
or that cannot be easily disposed of in television terms.
Such events challenge the notion of accepted values
at the mass or cultural level. They suggest that individual visions are important and that the audience
must come to terms with its own values if they apply
or do not apply to the subject at hand. The creation
of "real" content for television is crucial to this process. If we feel that the newscaster is announcing his
or her personal views within the context of "the"
news, we are uncomfortable. If an athlete's private
life clashes with his public image, we must react in
more complex ways. Similarly, the fictional structures
that we must now examine in the following chapters
allow for ambiguity and complexity in a less formulaic way than those forms we have discussed so far.

In varying ways, they, too, move us toward a more confusing experience. In doing so they prove that television is capable of creating works of art on its own terms which are comparable to fine works in other media. They prove that television cannot be explained in terms of a single type of entertainment, but provides a range of works rich and varied for its varied audiences. Many of these works remain highly popular, suggesting that the popular arts are capable of exceptional complexity on their own terms and fulfill numerous functions in a pluralistic society.

9

THE NEW SHOWS

"New" shows break old patterns of action, move toward varied value orientations, and refuse to indulge in the predictability of most television. They sometimes demand a new understanding of some visual techniques. Some are edited with a new sense of television narrative, rather than in a standard, cinematic manner. They carry with them a more sensitive attitude toward character, which in turn requires a more complex sort of acting. The writing of new shows is richer in image and tone than that common to familiar television shows. Ultimately, these factors prohibit the application of a single set of standards to television. Less dependent on formula and standardized action, these shows move farther along the continuum toward the "fine" arts. And though it is possible to point here to the same sort of audience education that has occurred with movies, it is more likely that television will begin to pay attention to the multiplicity of tastes within the mass as it develops specialized programming to meet many different needs and desires.

In a way, of course, there have always been "new" shows. The recent showing of a sequence of Sid Caesar productions in movie theaters can demonstrate the power of comic genius which asks an audience to participate in its antics rather than relax before them. "The Defenders," although highly formulaic in some respects, did ask, in the early sixties, that the audience consider moral, cultural, and social problems which could lead us into new ideas about assumed beliefs. "East Side, West Side," the story of a New York City social worker, used the acting abilities of George C. Scott in stories that reflected a realistic treatment of material not often seen on television. "Star Trek" moved toward a probing of our most unquestioned human and national attitudes, touched social issues, and even suggested strong remedies for many social problems. It was a self-conscious attempt to deal with controversial responses to accepted situations. It undercut these attempts by relying on a structure that caused it to resemble the most thoughtless of television adventure shows, but perhaps it was a mark of the time that even with this sort of formulaic conclusion the show still captured the imagination of a wide audience. That audience recognized the complexity of ideas built into the show, and it is often cited fondly as one of the few series that have dealt with large and multifaceted problems in a manner that approaches honesty.

In many ways, however, these shows were atypical. Some of them, such as "Star Trek," were not good as mass advertising vehicles, despite a large cult audience. Others, such as "East Side, West Side," though capable for a time of high ratings, were deemed too controversial. Some, like "The Defenders," managed to walk the tightrope of acceptability and remain models of good programming. All of them helped prepare artists and audiences for the major artistic breakthroughs of several recent shows.

"Laugh-In" became a part of NBC's mid-season replacement schedule in 1968. It was built on the popu-

larity of a few specials by hosts Dan Rowan and Dick
Martin, but its sudden and fantastic success was the
result of far more important ingredients. While the
two stars remained as the center of the show, their
function quickly became that of the perfectly appropriate personalities linking the rapid-fire segments of
this visually and conceptually complex show.

Visually the show was a collage, a kaleidoscope. Special effects caused the televised image to ripple onto
home receivers, to shatter and fade before our eyes.
Edited to run faster than anything previously seen on
television, juxtaposed segments were related only by
the style of the humor. Printed words sometimes
floated across the video image, forcing the audience
to read one-line puns as it simultaneously watched
the visual action and listened to the jokes of the performers. In many segments the background music was
loud, stopping abruptly as the audience listened,
watched, and read all at the same time. Filmed sequences were intercut with videotaped segments,
and movement from studio to location could occur
with no forewarning or apparent cause.

The fast pace and unusual editing of the show were
modified and somewhat softened by the highly repetitive nature of the sequence of events. Certain segments of the show appeared each week, and we could
look forward to the Party Scene, to Laugh-In Looks
at the News, a satirical poke at our conceptions of
"reality," or to the presentation of the irreverent Fly-
ing Fickle Finger of Fate Award.

The actors and actresses were just as important in
giving the show continuity as were the special sequences. Each week during the early years of the
show we waited eagerly for Judy Carne to have it
"socked to her." We could anticipate Joanne Worley's

fabled parodies of operatic singing. Even more crucial was the fact that many of these participants played multiple roles. Henry Gibson became famous as the "with it" minister and as the reciter of his own doggerel. Arty Johnson created the German soldier spying at the close of each show and the "dirty old man" who harassed Ruth Buzzi in one of her roles. Lily Tomlin developed several characters which became favorites of the audience, Ernestine, the telephone operator, and Edith Ann, the spoiled child, among them.

"Laugh-In's" exceptionally large cast, supplemented even further by the guests who appeared on each show, and its extra-rapid construction combined to make another special demand on the audience; every line was to be laughed at. These lines were quick and often tricky, a particular type of harsh satire, hardly ever built on rising action. Much of the humor was political or personal in nature and was directed toward personalities and institutions. Much of it satirized religious beliefs, while other parts attacked cultural beliefs and accepted notions. Favorite targets in these areas were Richard Nixon, Billy Graham, and John Wayne.

In another vein much of the humor was sexual in nature. Many of the jokes, particularly the puns, bordered as nearly as possible on traditional "dirty stories." Certain catchphrases and stylized lines such as "sock it to me" or "your Funk and Wagnalls," when used in specific contexts, became scatological in nature. Dick Martin was depicted throughout the show as a lecherous bachelor, and in the party sequence was frequently seen making suggestive propositions to beautiful women.

Structurally, the show's over-all appeal was based

on many of the same facets of television that we have
seen in other forms from situation comedy to police
series. Here, that similarity is expressed by John
Cawelti.

I also feel that the group goes beyond this level of
performers as people having a bright good time to
invoke a sense of the group as family. Dan Rowan
is the wise, kindly and tolerant father with his
clever bunch of kids, while Dick Martin is a scandal
and a delight to the rest of the family. This may
be a somewhat oversimplified way of describing the
quality of collective affection which the *Laugh-In*
performers project, but they are surely as persuasive
in manifesting a feeling of this sort as the more
heavy-handed image of a benevolent patriarchy
which Lawrence Welk made such an important
element of his variety show. This comparison makes
one want to speculate about changing images of the
American family and the way this imagery functions
in group performances on TV. . . . ["Performance
and Popular Culture," paper presented at the
Popular Culture Association Convention, Toledo,
Ohio, 1972, p. 7]

Since much of television has been discussed here
in terms of familial values, this sort of speculation is
indeed called for. Even so I would take issue with
Cawelti that the image here is of a large family. The
comparison with the Welk show is the perfect one,
however, for it points to "Laugh-In's" truly innovative
nature. Welk carefully modeled the show on the traditional family structure, so common to television.
"Laugh-In" turned the image into satire, and the feeling described by Cawelti is more appropriately defined
as the sort of "affection" found in an apartment complex devoted to the vigorous lives of "swinging

singles." This was made even more clear by "Laugh-In's" mock version of the "normal" American family. When they turned to this image, it was to present us with the Farkle family segment of their show. Another attack on traditional values, this bit pointed to sexual activity outside the family. As the Farkle children sat about the living room, grinning somewhat stupidly, we immediately recognized that they did not resemble their father, Fred Farkle, but rather his next door neighbor who was always present as "a part of the family."

Such segments fit the over-all design of the show and defined its power and popularity. They were clearly intended to shock, to challenge accepted values, to call certain beliefs into question. If, at a deep structural level, the reversed family values of "swinging singles," or the Farkle family, represented a continuing concern with familial units, they also reflected a deep and increasing dissatisfaction with conventional answers to family problems. In doing so they cut incisively not only into the cultural question but into television's pop answers as well. Both Lawrence Welk and "The Brady Bunch" were made to look somehow foolish by "Laugh-In's" criticism.

That criticism was always mock serious in tone, and we ultimately got no clear answers or profound alternatives from the show, even if we wanted them. One image made this particularly clear. During the party sequence of the show and at various points throughout other segments we frequently focused on quick cuts to the body of a go-go dancer. The girl wore a scanty bikini and on her body were painted slogans, words, phrases, puns, and designs. To the sound of rock the camera focused and blurred, zoomed in and out at a frantic pace, and panned the

entire body. At the same time the dancer dipped and
swirled in sensuous gyrations. As a result of the two
kinds of movement, it was difficult to follow the visual
series. It was nearly impossible to read the words, and
at times the entire process was visually and mentally
annoying. The eye was forced to move more rapidly
than usual if the words were to be read. More importantly, the eye was forced to move more quickly
in order to see any given portion of the nearly nude
body of the dancer. Hips and breasts, flat bare stom-
ach, and long legs enticed the audience for a longer
look at what tended to be more nudity than anything
previously presented on TV. But the camera pre-
vented the long-drawn-out, sensual look and forced
the glance, the blink. The camera created the titillation in much the same way that the humor titillated
us to consider social and cultural alternatives to the
easy answers usually seen on television.

Even if it remained at the titillating level, however,
one thing is certain. "Laugh-In" did make it necessary
for the audience to respond to the show in different
ways; its ideas were challenged whether or not its
behavior was changed. For some portions of the audience the shady jokes and sexual references were amusing but also embarrassing. If these viewers were somewhat uneasy, it was necessary for them to adjust. For
other viewers this same sort of adjustment was made
necessary because of the technical innovations of the
show. Accustomed to sitting passively as jokes were
told by stand-up comedians or performed by sitcom
characters, they could no longer fall into a state of
semiconsciousness without missing much of the show.
For still other viewers "Laugh-In" created this sort of
tension in a more complex way. Capable of accepting the challenge to values and of absorbing it at

a fast pace, these viewers could be disturbed when the show turned the cultural tables. Having been the butt of many favorite jokes, personalities such as Nixon, Graham, and Wayne suddenly appeared on "Laugh-In" and appeared to enjoy the experience thoroughly. Those who thought of the show as a politically or culturally iconoclastic exercise supporting their own point of view must have watched the warm welcome of such guests with some dismay.

In the last analysis it is difficult to say whether or not "Laugh-In" broke the mold of popular television art by forcing the audience out of accepted values and into a questioning attitude. Although much of its material and almost all of its tone were irreverent with regard to accepted cultural standards, it is also true that many of those standards were already being questioned at the time of its creation. It may also be true that there has always been a wider acceptance of sexual innuendo and political satire than has been recognized by the money-conscious television sponsors. In any case, the show was a major innovation both technically and conceptually. It contributed an awareness of the possibility for something that would bend the expectations that had so often been satisfied. While many shows would continue to offer the same sort of formulas, others would build on "Laugh-In's" ground breaking.

When their show went off the air in 1972, Rowan and Martin were quoted as saying that there was simply nothing left in America to make fun of. Given the abstract nature of their humor, the structure of the review rather than that of the narrative, this might have been the case. For the producers of "All in the Family," however, it does not seem so. This show, first programmed by CBS in 1971, has frequently been the center of controversy about television's role as mass entertainment. Patterned after the domestic comedy, it challenges every stereotype of that formula, and at times pushes to the edges of the most complex artistic productions. It is another mark of the deep cultural base of television that the innovations of "All in the Family" may be seen again as directly related to the family patterns established in more conventional forms of comedy.

The show opens with helicopter shots of New York City, and as they dwell on the Midtown towers, it is almost possible to think of entering one of the apartment buildings for an episode of "Family Affair" or some other soft domestic comedy. But we do not stay there. Instead, the shots move steadily through more and more middle-class neighborhoods and finally into the reaches of Queens where street after street is filled with lower-middle-class housing. Finally the door of one of the houses becomes the focal point of the camera, and we enter the home of the Bunkers.

Inside, the differences are as distinct as out. The furniture is not the plush modern with which television audiences have always been familiar. It is old, worn, without style. The comforts are those of use rather than of design, and the easy chair sits before the television set waiting for Archie to occupy it. The chair often becomes a sign of his position in the home, and any intruders are forced out of it. The dining area is in the living room. Upstairs the bedrooms are bastions of privacy, but as in any crowded situation privacy is often ignored. The bathroom—there is only one —is another point of contention, and serves both as a battleground for the two families in the home and as a symbol of Archie's social prudery. He does not allow anyone to mention "going to the bathroom."

The people fit the house. Archie is a laborer on a warehouse loading dock. His wife is uneducated beyond high school, plain, dressed in common clothes. Their daughter, Gloria, and her husband live with the parents. She is pretty, not overly bright. She plays for her father's attention and antagonizes him with her views. Michael, her husband, is a college student supported by his wife and her family. Their liberal attitudes are violently at variance with Archie's. So that they do not become too functional as speakers for a "correct" point of view, however, their views are stereotyped liberal attitudes not often reflective or individualistic.

Physically the show is an example of a way of life common to much of the audience. It stands in direct contradiction to the dreamlike world of most situation-domestic comedy. Rather than being a sample of the fantasy world of the American middle-class life, it is the representation of an actual world.

The action of this show turns on Archie's character. He is a bigot. He openly expresses his dislike for minority races, using the epithets known throughout the culture: kikes, wops, jigaboos, and jungle bunnies. He curses, he swears. He mispronounces some words and misuses others. He professes to be a conservative, and all of the stereotyped conservative issues become his special concern. This creates the "situation," of course, for he finds himself in direct conflict with Michael and Gloria on almost all political issues and on issues involving cultural norms. He is embarrassed by sex, by bodily functions of any sort. He is outraged by racial mingling for any purpose. Here, as in "Laugh-In," the profanity and the sexual innuendo keep the audience on edge. These devices have been uncommon on television, as have the realistic settings.

The one works with the other to create a sense of realism in Archie's world.

The controversy surrounding the show has been primarily concerned with whether or not it fosters and shows approval of bigotry and racism. For some viewers and critics, any show that enables the audience to laugh at such attitudes indicates that the audience can approve of the beliefs. For others it means that such attitudes are widespread and should be seen for what they are. Since almost every episode ends by making Archie the ultimate butt of the joke, goes this argument, viewers will laugh at the bigot rather than with him.

Both arguments oversimplify the show. They ignore the way in which certain devices, such as Archie's prudery or profanity, touch much of the audience. Many of the viewers are also reticent about sexual and physiological functions. Many of them swear or choose explicitly not to swear. All factors work as they did on "Laugh-In" to keep the audience tense and consequently more alert to the actual content of the show. Some judgment on the part of the audience is made necessary, a factor that is not at all important for most television shows, where judgment is written into a series of easy problems and simple resolutions are reached by the stock characters.

Also ignored is the sympathetic nature of the two central roles. Even when he is most cruel in his bigotry, Archie is depicted as a man who is produced by social and cultural conditions. He can be pitied for his views, but there is another side that calls for his defense. When he fears for his job and discriminates against racial minorities in order to protect it, he speaks for many people in the audience. When he is shown to suffer for these actions, he speaks for others. We are not allowed to rest with one-dimensional characters or situations, for the viewer who condemns Archie must also condemn the social structure that produces him, and some critical viewers are made uncomfortable by such an identification.

Similarly, Edith Bunker's role takes us into multiple areas of concern. On one level she is the feather-brained housewife, the "ding-bat" that Archie names her. But we frequently see her deep sense of compassion or her commonsense approach winning out over Archie's incredible boisterousness. He is made to look foolish beside her. But again there is a double reversal. This picture of the housewife, the backbone of the family, subtly becomes a repressive argument for maintaining the feather-brained persona. It is demeaning to many women to see such a façade, one that argues keeping one's place in order to hold the family together.

These complexities add to what may have become the most complex of plots in television. While the show established an early sense of the provocative, it has succeeded in going beyond that with a continual attempt to move in new directions. In the closing episodes of its second season audiences saw what promised a new sense of television art.

In one episode Archie and his family argue about the appearance and activity of two refrigerator repairmen, one white, one black. Archie remembers the black man as a violent revolutionary, the white as a mobster. His own actions, depicted in flashback, are presented as mild, cowed, polite, and subdued. For other members of the family the memories are quite different, and as we see each version in flashback, we are offered a comic television version of *Rashomon*.

The nature of reality is defined by each participant's perceptions. The perceptions are molded by influences outside the individuals. Just as Archie distorts in one direction, Michael and Gloria distort in another. Edith, as usual, remembers what "really" happened, and the other characters have their comeuppance.

In another, stronger, episode, Gloria comes home shattered, having been molested on her way from work. She argues with her family about whether or not to report the incident to the police. Archie and Michael, for their own male-oriented father and husband reasons, say that she must report. Fearing notoriety and embarrassment, she hesitates and goes into the kitchen to talk to her mother. In the meantime a policeman arrives and gives Archie and Michael some idea of what the situation will be like if she does decide to testify. She will indeed be accused of provocation, of poor character, and so on, because that is the way in which rape cases are handled. In the kitchen Edith has convinced Gloria to report in order to protect potential victims, and when she comes into the living room, she is met with the stubborn refusal of the males to consent to this action. She is left not knowing what to do and the camera freezes her anguish in close-up. The audience is forced to consider this social issue on its own terms, within its own value structure.

A third episode is more brutal than either of these. A swastika is painted on Archie's door by mistake, having been intended for the door of a Jewish school board member who also lives on the street. A young man comes to Archie's aid as the leader of the "Hebrew Defense League." He argues for militant action and finds a friend in Archie, who has nevertheless managed to get in a variety of "Jewish" jokes. Michael

sees both of them as fools, blind to the results of violence. As the young man leaves and goes to his car,
the house is rocked by an explosion. We expect some
sort of humorous ending, common to the situation
comedy and common to this show. Instead, Archie
and his family look out of their front door and see the
remains of the man's car. "My God," says Archie, "it's
Paul. They blew him up in his car." The camera freezes
the contorted faces of the four characters, framed in
the doorway of their lower-middle-class home. Without resolution, without explanation, without the theme
music, the titles of the show roll over their faces, and
the audience is left once again to consider the meaning of the episode. A cardinal rule for formulaic television has been that people should not be killed in
situation comedies. But "All in the Family" has refused to accept the conventional categories and
formulas. Mixing and choosing on its own, it has
pushed to the limits of comedy, turning wild humor
into sudden bitter reality. Such jolts grow directly
out of the kind of tension created by profanity and
sex jokes. They wrench the audience out of compla-
cency. Doubtless, such episodes are not overly popular. They are confusing and annoying. But they
clearly demonstrate that social commentary can
create new forms of television and that television is
capable of complexity in its entertainment.

Because this series, like most of television, refuses
to develop a linear continuity in which such events
are remembered and referred to in later episodes,
Archie's character does not change as a result of these
drastic moments. Perhaps, in the context of the show,
that is an advantage. If he should suddenly shift his
view, modify his character, more would be lost than
gained. For Archie does have a sort of symbolic prob-

ability. He finds his life interwoven with those of all sorts of other characters, and his predictable reactions form a catalyst. Any reaction is forced onto the audience, rather than turned back into the series.

The initial fears of sponsors and network executives, fears that the American audience would be unable to accept forceful social commentary in a realistic format, were proven false. It follows, inevitably, that the successes of "Laugh-In" and "All in the Family" would become the temptation of other producers. The result is a spate of "socially conscious" comedies, some successful, some horrible failures.

"Sanford and Son," like "All in the Family," is a copy of a British production. It purports to offer us a realistic look at lower-class black life. The central characters are a junk dealer and his son who exhibit all sorts of generational differences. So far the show has failed to come up to the standards of the more active productions, serving mainly as a vehicle for the brilliant one-line delivery of the star of the show, Redd Foxx.

"Maude," developed as a companion to "All in the Family," has done better. Maude is a cousin of Edith Bunker's, the perfect liberal counterpart to Archie's conservatism. She, too, is a parody, and her weaknesses demonstrate the real bite of the show. Occasionally, the producers break new ground with this series. Maude decided, in a famous two-part episode during the 1972–73 season, to have an abortion. The 1973–74 season opened with an examination of her husband's alcoholism. Generally, even with such material, the show manages to lighten the audience's burden in some way and seems unwilling to offer the unresolved tension of the parent show.

These two shows are essentially copies of "All in

the Family." One other show, however, has created a format and an attitude of its own, which moves farther along the direction pointed by the Bunkers. "M*A*S*H" is historical in setting; its action takes place during the Korean War, in the combat zone. The family structure is here, but again it is not a biological family. Rather, we have a set of characters forced into deep human relationships because they are serving in a field hospital, isolated from other groups. The central characters make their lives bearable by circumventing U. S. Army regulations. This, in itself, sets the tone of critical commentary. One of the characters portrays a pseudo-transvestite, hoping for a psychological discharge. Other characters openly engage in extramarital sex. Beneath the raucous humor lies the war in which they are directly involved, and some of the grimmest jokes take place in the operating room.

The title shots make it plain that these characters are often in anguish over their inability to heal the maimed soldiers who come into the hospital. But the war continues indefinitely. The cast of characters, then, has modified its values into an upside-down world, reminiscent of the novel *Catch-22*. Their humor is a means of retaining sanity in an insane world of war. The audience is caught between its laughter and its realization—gently prodded when things get too lighthearted—that the war provides the theater for the humor. Even so, the choice has been made to emphasize the comedy and to reduce the specific social commentary. This show and "All in the Family" are strong indications that comedy is now the chief vehicle for social criticism on television, a belief that is self-consciously shared by writers and producers of "Maude's" alcoholism segment.

The authors of the segment, Bob Schiller and Bob Weiskopf, who are also story editors, with Alan J. Levitt, for "Maude," say it was one of their toughest writing assignments. The script, like all "Maude" scripts, was a team effort, involving executive producer Norman Lear, producer Rod Parker, and script editor Budd Grossman, all of whom are writers as well. More than three months were spent on the script, involving about 10 rewrites.

"We did it because we think it says something that needed saying, and happily, the studio audience watching the show being taped went along with us," says Schiller, adding that their reaction was an indication that viewers at home would also accept it.

"What we wanted to say," Schiller continues, "was, hey America, we're all drinking too much, and it's getting out of hand. We show them that if it can happen to a lovable character like Walter Findlay, and he can face up to his problem, then a lot of other Americans with the same problem can face it, too. . . ."

Schiller and Weiskopf adamantly disagree with those critics who feel the comedy format is not the best method for dealing with controversy. They point out that throughout the history of theater, going back to the ancient Greeks, the comedy form was most often chosen to introduce a topic of public interest.

. . . "There are a lot of funny things in the 'Maude' script on Walter's problem," they say. "But we never give the impression that the disease of alcoholism is funny, because it isn't. It's deadly serious, and that's the whole point. [CBS press release, August 1973]

This is indeed the point. But traditionally it has been avoided by popular television, the chief concern of which has been the service of entertainment which purposely removes its audience from "serious" concerns. We have also seen that even in dramatic productions, where serious concerns have been the major subject matter, they have been dealt with in a manner that submerges their ambiguous nature in a mass of culturally acceptable solutions.

Just as comedy has become a vehicle for social criticism, however, television drama has increasingly begun to explore social and personal issues that cannot be resolved easily or quickly, maintaining at the same time a sense of popular entertainment that can attract a mass audience. In 1968, for example, there appeared on American television a British import called "The Prisoner." Starring Patrick McGoohan, it was ostensibly a continuation of an earlier series called "Secret Agent." The "prisoner" seemed to be the "secret agent" who had been forcibly retired by his superiors because he had come to know too much of his ugly business and was disillusioned with it. As a consequence, he was drugged and spirited away to an island filled with similar "retired" agents. The series was premised on the man's desire to escape, but what made the show maddeningly interesting was the depiction of the island as a utopian paradise. No need was left unattended, no concern unanswered. The turn, of course, came when one realized that the island was an Orwellian utopia, filled with continual electronic monitoring and maintained by a restriction of movement. To put it another way, the only need or consideration left unfulfilled was human freedom.

What makes the show important for television's increasing concern with important issues is the fact that it offered a complete reversal of all the traditional values of popular adventure. The bad guys were those who created and supplied the paradise. The good guy continually tried to escape paradise rather than revel in it. With equal regularity he failed in his attempts, and the bad guys triumphed as he was put once again into his elegantly appointed prison. Every episode ended with the remarkably graphic effect of bars clanging shut over the face of the prisoner.

It does not call for great exaggeration to see the entire series as a metaphor for the contemporary condition as often described by more philosophical thinkers. Prisoner of systems he does not understand but that cater to his physical needs, modern man is reduced to a cipher. (Similarly, in "The Prisoner" inhabitants of the island are known only by code number rather than by name.) He is unable to pin down the forces that keep him in check, that prevent his total freedom. In spite of this he is better provided for, more "comfortable," than human beings have ever been before.

I am not suggesting here that the television audience of this popular show sat in living rooms throughout America and discussed the metaphysical implications of the plight of its hero. But by working within all the constraints of the popular arts the show did manage to create a new form of spy show which reversed and questioned all the assumptions of that form. In doing so it paralleled developments in contemporary espionage literature. At the same time it managed to satisfy the entertainment needs of a large audience.

A similar show, in conception if not in content, appeared in 1969. It was American-produced and for its central character had a motorcycle wanderer called Bronson. In many ways this show, "Then Came Bronson," was an updated version of "Route 66." In the tradition of the wanderer, its hero was a young,

completely unattached, and only moderately motivated young man. In the pilot episode Bronson's best
friend is killed, and he sets out across America in
search of some sort of meaning.

The title shots of each episode included a sequence
that set the tone for the series. Bronson pulls to a stop
for a traffic light. Beside him, in what is obviously a
family sedan, sits a man on his way home from work.
The man wears a suit and tie; a hat is pushed to the
back of his head. He looks out of his window at Bronson and asks, "Where're you headed?" Bronson replies that he will go wherever the road takes him.
"Man, I wish I were you," says the businessman. For
this he receives Bronson's advice, "Well, hang in
there." The light changes and the two drive away—
down different roads. The camera pulls back for a
series of long shots in which Bronson is seen driving
his motorcycle across bridges at Big Sur, over beaches
in the golden sun, around mountains and across
deserts.

The lyrical quality established in these shots is continued in many individual episodes, some of which are
far more poetic than narrative. In one episode Bronson drives into a mountain meadow and stops at an
old farmhouse. The house is occupied by an old
woman, somewhat senile, and in need of a companion. Bronson spends a few days with her. She relives
much of her life through the stories she tells him, and
in a lovely fantasy sequence sees Bronson as her long-
dead husband. They dance, dreamlike, and she tells
him of the balls she attended and of their life in this
land of wild beauty. In the end she dies. Bronson has
learned much about life from her.

In an even less-structured episode Bronson is on his
way to visit an old friend who is a forest ranger in a

national park. Unwilling to follow the prepared course of the roads, he decides to ride through the great forest. He gets lost, and in the difficulties encountered has an almost mystic experience. He moves close to the deer and the other animals. He is in awe of the massive trees which surround him. In one sequence he wanders on foot around the trees, and the camera offers us fish-eye shots of the towering giants. Bronson weeps from weariness, panic, and joy. In the end he stumbles out of the forest into his friend's cabin grounds. Bronson's experience has been both ecstatic and frightening. He has learned something about self-sufficiency and something about man's place in Nature as well. He is stronger and more humble.

It is this focus, finally, that distinguishes "Then Came Bronson" from its predecessors and other contemporary shows of its type. Bronson is not the wanderer who encounters other characters and brings resolution to their lives and problems. His interactions are almost always inner-directed, even when he does help other people. He is the focus of the show. His development, what he learns, is supposed to touch us, and that asks a great deal of the television audience. There was nothing special about Bronson other than his questioning of established and easily accepted values. One could not assume that any problem he encountered would be solved by the end of the hour. If "Route 66" was the outgrowth and acceptable version of *On the Road,* "Bronson's" parent was *Easy Rider,* and the strong resemblance to the counter-cultural heroes and minimally defined action hastened the show's death at the end of a single season.

As much as any other factor, the show's lack of resolution became a negative factor. It worked within the one-hour format which carries all the connotations

of hard-edged endings, powerful concluding statements, or moral and social values. Bronson offered
none of these. But 1969 was also the year in which
television did find a form that could continue without
full resolution, that could offer dramatic continuity,
complex characterization, and conceptual ambiguity.
It could do all this and still attract a major audience.
The form was much like that of the novel, which also
happened to be that of the soap opera. The show was
"The Forsyte Saga."

Critics were quick to praise the presentation and
saw that there was something there that was not often
offered by television. The appeal is defined here by
Margot Hentoff.

One of the things which distinguishes good bad
fiction from insufferable bad fiction is that, in the
former, the characters, however stock, hold our
interest. We like knowing what they do. The *Forsyte*
novels are good bad fiction at its best—admirably
suited to the reduction of television since there is
little complexity to be lost in the transition. In
fact, the shrinking effect makes Galsworthy seem
far leaner and more witty than he was. [*Vogue*,
January 1, 1970, p. 84]

Caring about characters is one of the essential elements in art that moves beyond the formulaic. With
the turn to a continuing series with continuing and
developing characters, television tapped this central
point. Characters could now change. They could offer
different points of view. They were not immortally pre-
served because of the star system or because of their
heroic nature. Soap opera had known this for some
time, had known that there was a special appeal in
characters that could live lives of their own. The BBC
producers reinvented the principle of the soaps when

they applied it to forms not defined by characters and events that are common soap opera stereotypes.

One of the things made clear by the "Saga" was the appeal of the period piece for television audiences. Again, Hentoff catches the point. "Weekly, we watch the fall of the Empire in the falling away of the Forsytes from the original family purpose of unity and accumulation. And weekly, like naïfs, we become convinced that both disintegrations are to be mourned. We are caught up in the Galsworthy point of view" (ibid.). It is somewhat strange to hear this term, point of view, this defining characteristic of the novel, applied to television. But it is appropriate. In many series the BBC has proven that television can accurately capture a novelist's point of view. More importantly, they have proved that television series can create their own points of view in works patterned on the novel. They could turn to material that appealed to an audience's desire for historical emphasis, in which characters were created for concern, in which all the elements of popular excitement could be captured. In these new types of shows could be discovered the possibilities for the medium's own greater creativity.

In 1971 the BBC produced "The Six Wives of Henry VIII." Like the "Saga," it became an immediate success in England and in other countries. Each of the six episodes of the series centered around Henry's relationships with one of his wives. The world that surrounded those relationships became equally developed. Court intrigues, international relations both civil and ecclesiastical, the mixes among them—all these offered the audience a rare glimpse at a moment of history. At the center of the work was the character of Henry, who, like the Forsytes, made us care for his life. The performance by Keith Michell was a *tour de force*. As we watched the aging Henry grow fatter and more feeble, his personal life and his attitudes moved more and more to the foreground and the drama focused on the man.

Even so, the drama was enhanced by the acting of each of the characters, those who continued and those who found themselves beheaded or otherwise disposed of at the end of single episodes. Camera work explored the interiors of castles, creeping around columns in moments of whispered plans, following characters into dungeons. The richness of court activity was brought to life.

This series was quickly followed by another devoted to the life of Elizabeth I. The central performance, by Glenda Jackson, rivaled that of Michell as Henry. Of crucial importance to both series is the fact that the central characters are followed throughout critical periods of their lives, but the interest is heightened by the fact that we follow each of them to their deaths. Henry and Elizabeth age as we watch them. The aging is not pretty. In the final episode of the Elizabeth study, the dying queen resembles a skeleton in clown face, her own face a thick mask of cosmetics, her hair a faulty wig. She takes days in dying. The camera moves slowly about the palace while she sits or stands, knowing what is happening. The stillness and the silence—so contrary to conventional television—act as metaphor. An age is ending, and this is conveyed to the audience by symbol rather than with the easy definition so common to most television shows. The magnitude of Elizabethan England has been defined here by the character of the queen, and this intimacy of the character study is appropriate to television. The continuing series creates a sense of probability for the actions, and a texture of life is developed.

The BBC has continued its run of television successes with video adaptations of works by major and minor authors. Henry James's "The Spoils of Poynton" and *The Golden Bowl* have been made into series, as have Balzac's *Père Goriot* and *Cousin Bette* and Dostoevski's *The Gambler*. In the classic tradition of the mystery story we have seen Wilkie Collins' *The Moonstone*, and in the pattern of TV's reliance on juvenile appeal, Thomas Hughes's *Tom Brown's School Days*. In addition to the adaptations, exceptional work has also been done by commercial British television in original television series such as *Upstairs, Downstairs*, an intricate study of British society of the Edwardian Era.

Three other series, one British and two American, deserve special attention, for they all represent departures and new directions for television. All of them use the techniques described so far and manipulate them in various ways. The British production is "The Search for the Nile." The breadth of this series lies in the exploration of the Victorian sensibility and surveys the consuming desire of a whole generation to discover the source of the Nile. Its depth comes from the focus on the experience of Sir Richard Burton, and in depicting him as the prototypical rebellious spirit, lays open the explorer's mind. The search for the source of the great river, for everyone except Burton, becomes a metaphor for colonialism, and the applications of the white man's culture can be seen in varying modes, from the missionary zeal and compassion of David Livingstone to the repacious attitudes of John Speke and the later Henry Stanley.

A great portion of the series is given over to the

exploration of these motivations. As Burton is forced to live out most of his life in the bitter knowledge that his work is unrecognized and unappreciated, we sense the struggle of the individual against a prevailing set of cultural norms. "The Search for the Nile" offers dramas within dramas: Burton against the culture, against Speke, against public opinion, against his wife. Stanley's devotion to Livingstone, Livingstone's devotion to Africa, the natives' love for Livingstone—all these point to deep and abiding human considerations.

As the great explorers die, we feel the death of an age and an idea, as with the endings of Henry and Elizabeth. The series appropriately closes with scenes of Richard Burton's work going up in flames. Following his death his wife chose to expurgate his life by destroying records of his work in erotic art and anthropological speculation. The camera closes in on the curling, burning pages, and another world drifts away. The adventure and excitement that so often define television have been shown in this series, not as the result of some formulaic motivation, but as one of the driving concerns of humanity. We need not go to the detectives to find a world that takes us into exotic locations and physical challenge. The world of the explorers and their strange psychology will do it as well. When produced in the way that "The Search for the Nile" was produced, they do it better. History becomes the subject matter for television.

"An American Family" moves to the opposite end of the spectrum, offering us contemporary life rather than history, documentary rather than fictionalized selection, and "everyday people" rather than explorers. The series was the idea of producer Craig Gilbert, who planned it as an exploration of contemporary American problems and values. His plan was to focus on a typical American family in an attempt to explain many of the tensions that seemed to be pulling it apart. In the midst of his filming, the family did come apart, and the production of the series developed into a controversy still unsettled. The significance of the series lies in its reliance on a set of cultural images and attitudes common both to fictional television and to "real" life.

In many ways the William Loud family, chosen by Gilbert to be representative, resembles the families we see most nights on television. They live in California. They are affluent. The children are rock musicians, dancers, concerned with school, their friends, their pets. Their problems are with money, cars, part-time work. To the degree that they see themselves in this way, and to the degree that they play for the ever-present cameras, they become part of television's fantasy world. As the eldest son put it, "Everyone wants to be the star of their own television series, don't they?" But as the series progresses, we see more and more differences between the families of TV and the families of reality. The Loud children are not the slick, witty group we find in "The Brady Bunch," nor are they the classy professionals of "The Partridge Family." Their adolescent difficulties are not resolved with the ease of "Father Knows Best." Importantly, they exhibit little of the exuberance of those fictional groups. Instead, their actions appear frantic at one moment, deadly dull in the next.

From another angle we see the roots of soap opera here. As the Louds experience problems with drinking, sex, infidelity, homosexuality, and ennui, all of the families of the soaps rise before us. The high point of the series, as in a developing soap opera subplot, is the discovery of impending divorce. Even so, there is the same sense of flatness in their lives that would be alleviated in the soaps by constant discovery of new complications. Each moment in the lives of the Louds is not equally important, as it seems to be in the soaps. There are few connections with other individuals; there is little sense of causality. We remain enclosed with the Louds in their expensive house or in their hotel rooms or in automobiles.

The gap between television and the Louds' version of the television family is a large one. It is easy to understand, if they are typical, why we as a culture have created the more pleasant version of the American family. It is also easy to understand why no real family can stand up to that idealization. The Louds charged that their family, for all its troubles, was not accurately represented by Gilbert's documentary. It is likely that any other version of their lives would have been equally misleading. The series attempted to explore some of our deepest cultural values and clearly demonstrated the interrelation between the values as we see them on television and express them in our own lives.

"An American Family" and a number of the other series we have examined have relied on the adaptation of historical moments or on documentaries of contemporary events for their subject matter. Others have adapted novels, again relying on a sense of the past for part of their appeal. Television has created its own historical fiction, however, in "The Waltons." In this series we return to the American Depression of the 1930s. Unlike "Search for the Nile" or "Elizabeth I," which depend on the lives of flamboyant individuals for the probing of cultural tensions, "The Waltons" explores stability within a culture by focusing on a family of the most unpretentious persons. The Waltons live in West Virginia. They are a farm family, a large group made up of three generations. Their troubles are caused in part by historical and social circumstances. But the economic difficulties of the Depression serve only to bring us to deeper understanding of the human conflicts.

The children are the focus of the show, and John Boy, the oldest, is the central character. He is an aspiring writer, and it is from his point of view that the stories are told. His sensibilities enable us to share the experiences of the family. Most episodes depend on some sort of generational conflict and are resolved by reaffirming the values of the family. They are also supported by other dramatic devices which make us aware that these children are different from the tyrants of contemporary situation-domestic comedy.

In one segment, for example, a wandering writer stays with the family in exchange for work. He regales John Boy with tales of the famous people he has known, of New York and the other cities he has seen. He offers the mystique of the writer as a way of life and speaks of the "one big story" that a man must seek, even if it means cutting himself off from his family. Finally, through a moment of crisis, John Boy learns that his family is his greatest asset, that he has let them down by listening to the romantic notions of the writer. The writer, too, confesses that there is little to what he has said. His own life has been wasted in wandering and in the telling of all his tales. He has written little. He encourages John Boy to stay where he is and diligently practice his craft.

A summary of the story is maudlin. But because we care for these people, it is saved from that. The elements of the production cause us to care for the individuals rather than for the resolution of tension inherent in a formula. The episodic structure of the program is balanced by the fact that the family continues to change. The children age, they face different sorts of problems. The characters are allowed to develop so that there is a sense of probability rather than predictability in their actions. The plots are seriously based on human experience rather than in the social stereotypes of most television shows.

"The Waltons," more than the British productions, returns us to the central issue of popular art. The show is rooted in American culture. Its images and symbols are developments of many of those we have already examined. It is a family show. The father and mother are traditional in their conservative attitudes. The show is built around problems, and the problems are always solved. It does not choose, ultimately, to question social or cultural values, though they may be rigorously examined in the course of an episode. Neither, however, does "The Waltons" offer the unquestioning acceptance of traditional American television formulas. Those shows are based on values similar to the ones found in "The Waltons," but the values are only implied. They are submerged in fantasy-like mixtures of fatherly cowboys and detectives, country doctors in modern dress, compassionate legal counselors, and parents with a magical sense of what is necessary to solve human problems. In "The Waltons" these values are called to the surface to be dealt with explicitly. Such an exploration of traditional American values and attitudes is highly self-conscious, as is evidenced by the attitude of the executive producer of the show, Earl Hamner.

We are in agony as a people. We desperately want to believe that our heritage is a proud one and that

we can survive the present disillusionment and
doubt. We have discarded the old values and have
found nothing to take their place. We are alone
and afraid and we need a security. That is why I
believe "The Waltons" have struck such a deep
response in the viewing public. They are sick of
vulgarity and violence, of suggestive dialogue, so-
called sensational subject matter, shallow plots, one-
dimensional characters and the pap and pulp
they are offered. They are hungry for affirmation
that what life has taught them is viable, vital and
affirmative. What the audience needs is some
sense of values to sustain them, some anchor to keep
them afloat through the present turmoil. I believe
we are not only bringing our audience entertainment, but some hope that if we once endured a
Depression, then it is possible we might endure
and survive this present test of the fabric of this
justly proud country. [Acceptance Speech, Man of
the Year Award, National Association of Television
Program Executives Conference, February 1974.
Quoted in *Facts, Figures & Film,* March 1974,
p. 29.]

Such a position suggests that the unself-conscious application of traditional values to medical, legal, social,
family, criminal, or Western problems is not sufficient.
The television audience is aware that such applications are fantastic, that there are no immediate and
magical solutions to current problems taken from their
experience.

The plots of "The Waltons," even as they reaffirm
these values, examine them in a historical context.
They suggest that while these beliefs are indeed the
ones to which we should return, such a return will
not make life easier. Learning to live with these attitudes is, for the Walton family, costly. Every lesson

absorbed by the adolescents leads them closer to the painful realization that there are no easy answers. Each solution forces the parents to realize that they must someday lose their children. The third generation watches, a second set of parents, knowing that they are seeing old mistakes played out, old problems faced anew. Most importantly, "The Waltons" reminds us that in facing these eternal issues there are no heroes; although a problem may be solved by John Boy, Daddy, or Mama, through it they learn a proper humility. This, then, is the new domestic drama. It builds on domestic comedy and the tragic soap opera, uniting both elements in a satisfying formula that can stand as a true television innovation.

The excellence of "The Waltons" and of the other new shows is, in part, the result of a growing sense that television can and does organize and arrange fictional material in forms of its own. It need not be seen solely as a transmission device which presents the traditional detective, Western, melodrama, and comedy of other forms. The newer shows do not relinquish the elements tried and proven in more formulaic presentation. Indeed, they can be seen as formulas themselves. What they suggest is a range of quality within television comparable to the range within other media. Fully to understand the possibilities, we can look more closely at the devices with which television creates its own versions of popular art.

10

TOWARD A TELEVISION AESTHETIC

Defining television as a form of popular art might lead one to ignore the complex social and cultural relationships surrounding it. In his book *Open to Criticism,* Robert Lewis Shayon, former television critic for *The Saturday Review,* warns against such a view.

To gaze upon this dynamic complexity and to delimit one's attention to merely the aesthetic (or any other single aspect of it) is to indulge one's passion for precision and particularity (an undeniable right) —but in my view of criticism it is analogous to flicking a piece of lint off a seamless garment.

   The mass media are phenomena that transcend even the broad worlds of literature. They call for the discovery of new laws, new relationships, new insights into drama, ritual and mythology, into the engagement of minds in a context where psychological sensations are deliberately produced for non-imaginative ends, where audiences are created, cultivated and maintained for sale, where they are trained in nondiscrimination and hypnotized by the mechanical illusion of delight. When the symbols that swirl about the planet Earth are manufactured by artists who have placed their talents at the disposition of salesmen, criticism must at last acknowledge that "literature" has been transcended and that the dialectics of evolutionary action have brought the arts to a new level of practice and significance.
[Boston, 1971, pp. 48–49]

What I have tried to suggest in the previous chapters is that humanistic analysis, when used to explore aesthetic considerations in the popular arts such as television, can aid directly in that "discovery of new laws, new relationships, new insights into drama, ritual and mythology," which Shayon calls for. In doing so it is necessary to concentrate on the entertaining works themselves, rather than on the psychological effects of those works on and within the mass audience. In those areas the social scientific methodologies may be more capable of offering meaningful results. But we should also remember that most of the works we have dealt with are highly formulaic in nature, and if we think of formula, in John Cawelti's words, as "a model for the construction of artistic works which synthesizes several important cultural functions," then it is possible to see how the aesthetic point of view and the social scientific point of view might supplement one another in a fuller attempt to discover the total meaning of the mass media.

Television is a crucially important object of study not only because it is a new "form," a different "medium," but because it brings its massive audience into a direct relationship with particular sets of values and attitudes. In the previous chapter, where we examined works that are less formulaic, we should still be able to recognize the direct connection, in terms of both values and the techniques of presenting them, with more familiar television entertainment. In those newer shows, where the values may become more ambiguous, more individualized, we find an extension and a development of popular television rather than a distinct new form of presentation. The extension and development have demonstrated that even in the more complex series, popularity need not be sacrificed.

To the degree that the values and attitudes of all these shows are submerged in the contexts of dramatic presentation, the aesthetic understanding of television is crucial. We have looked closely at the formulas that most closely identify television entertainment. We have been able to see how those formulas affect what has been traditionally thought of as nondramatic entertainment or as factual information. We have determined some of the values presented in each of the formulas in terms of their embodiment in certain character types, patterns of action, and physical environment. In approaching an aesthetic understanding of TV the purpose should be the description and definition of the devices that work to make television one of the most popular arts. We should examine the common elements that enable television to be seen as something more than a transmission device for other forms. Three elements seem to be highly developed in this process and unite, in varying degree, other aspects of the television aesthetic. They are intimacy, continuity, and history.

The smallness of the television screen has always been its most noticeable physical feature. It means something that the art created for television appears on an object that can be part of one's living room, exist as furniture. It is significant that one can walk around the entire apparatus. Such smallness suits television for intimacy; its presence brings people into the viewer's home to act out dramas. But from the beginning, because the art was visual, it was most commonly compared to the movies. The attempts to marry old-style, theater-oriented movies with television are stylistic failures even though they have proven to be a financial success. Television is at its best when it offers us faces, reactions, explorations of emotions registered by human beings. The importance is not placed on the action, though that is certainly vital as stimulus. Rather, it is on the reaction to the action, to the human response.

An example of this technique is seen in episode twelve of Alistair Cooke's "America: A Personal History." In order to demonstrate the splendor of a New England autumn, Cooke first offers us shots of expansive hillsides glowing with colored trees. But to make his point fully he holds a series of leaves in his hand. He stands in the middle of the forest and demonstrates with each leaf a later stage in the process from green to brown, stages in the process of death. The camera offers a full-screen shot of Cooke's hand portraying the single leaves. The importance of this scene, and for the series, is that Cooke insists on giving us a personal history. We are not so much concerned with the leaves themselves, but with the role they play in Cooke's memories of his early years in America. To make his point immediate, he makes sure that we see what he wants us to see about the autumnal color. The point about the process of death is his, not one that we would come to immediately, on our own, from viewing the leaves.

Commenting on the scene, Cooke praised his cameraman, Jim McMillan. It was McMillan, he said, who always insisted on "shooting for the box," or filming explicitly for television. Such filming is necessary in the series if Cooke's personal attitudes are to be fully expressed visually as well as in his own prose. (Alistair Cooke, concluding comments at a showing of episode twelve of "America: A Personal History" at the Maryland Institute College of Art, Baltimore, Maryland, April 1973)

Such use of technique is highly self-conscious. More

popular television, however, has always used exactly the same sense of intimacy in a more unconscious fashion. It is this sense that has done much of the transforming of popular formulas into something special for television. As our descriptions have shown, the iconography of rooms is far more important to television than is that of exterior locations. Most of the content of situation comedies, for example, takes place in homes or in offices. Almost all that of domestic comedy takes place indoors, and problems of space often lead to or become the central focus of the show. Even when problems arise from "outdoor" conflicts—can Bud play football if his mother fears for his safety—are turned into problems that can be dealt with and solved within the confines of the living room or kitchen.

Mysteries often take us into the offices of detectives or policemen and into the apartments and hideouts of criminals. In some shows, such as "Ironside," the redesigning of space in keeping with the needs of the character takes on special significance. Ironside requests and receives the top floor of the police headquarters building. In renovating that space he turns it not only into an office but into a home as well. His personal life is thereby defined by his physical relationship to his profession and to the idea of fighting crime. He inhabits the very building of protection. He resides over it in a godlike state that fits his relationship to the force. The fact that it is his home also fits him to serve as the father figure to the group of loyal associates and tempers the way in which he is seen by criminals and by audience. Similarly, his van becomes an even more confined space, also a home, but defined by his handicap. It is the symbol of his mobile identity as well as of his continued personal life.

Such observations would be unimportant were it not for the fact that as we become more intimately introduced to the environment of the detective we become equally involved with his personality. It is the character of the detective, as we have seen, that defines the quality of anticrime in his or her show. The minor eccentricities of each character, the private lives of the detectives, become one of the focal points of the series in which they appear. It is with the individual attitudes that the audience is concerned, and the crimes are defined as personal affronts to certain types of individuals.

Nowhere is this emphasis more important than in the Westerns. In the Western movie, panorama, movement, and environment are crucial to the very idea of the West. The films of John Ford or Anthony Mann consciously incorporate the meaning of the physical West into their plots. It may be that no audience could ever visually grasp the total expanse of land as depicted in full color, but this is part of the meaning of the West. The sense of being overwhelmed by the landscape helps to make clear the plight of the gunfighter, the farmer, the pioneer standing alone against the forces of evil.

On television this sense of expansiveness is meaningless. We can never sense the visual scope of the Ponderosa. The huge cattle herds that were supposed to form the central purpose for the drovers of "Rawhide" never appeared. In their place we were offered stock footage of cattle drives. A few cattle moved into the tiny square and looked, unfortunately, like a few cattle. The loneliness of the Kansas plains, in the same way, has never properly emerged as part of the concept of "Gunsmoke."

What has emerged in place of the "sense" of the physical West is the adult Western. In this form, perfected by television, we concentrate on the crucial human problems of individuals. One or two drovers gathered by the campfire became the central image of "Rawhide." The relationship among the group became the focus. Ben Cartwright and his family were soon involved in innumerable problems that rose out of their personal conflicts and the conflicts of those who entered their lives. Themes of love and rebellion, of human development and moral controversy, were common on the show until its demise. On "Have Gun—Will Travel" Paladin's business card was thrust into the entire television screen, defining the meaning of the show as no panoramic shot could. This importance of the enclosed image is made most clear in "Gunsmoke." The opening shots of the original version concentrated on the face of Matt Dillon, caught in the dilemma of killing to preserve justice. The audience was aware of the personal meaning of his expression because it literally filled the screen, and the same sorts of theme have always dominated the program content. Even when landscape and chase become part of the plot, our attention is drawn to the intensely individual problems encountered, and the central issue becomes the relationships among individuals.

This physical sense of intimacy is clearly based in the economic necessities of television production. It is far more reasonable, given budgetary restraints, to film sequences within permanent studio sets than on location, even when the Western is the subject. But certainly the uses of intimacy are no longer exclusively

based on that restriction. The soap operas, most finan-
cially restricted of all television productions, have developed the idea from the time when audiences were
made to feel as if they were part of a neighborhood
gossiping circle until today, when they are made to
feel like probing psychiatrists. Similarly, made-for-
television movies reflect this concern and are often
edited to heighten the sense of closeness. A greater
sense of the importance of this concept is found in
those shows and series that develop the idea of intimacy as a conceptual tool. It becomes an object of
study, a value to be held. In such cases the union of
form and content leads to a sense of excellence in
television drama.

The situation comedies such as "All in the Family,"
"Maude," "Sanford and Son," and "M*A*S*H" have
turned the usual aspects of this formula into a world
of great complexity. As we have seen, their themes
are often directed toward social commentary. The
comments can succeed only because the audience is
aware of the tightly knit structures that hold the families together. It is our intimate knowledge of their
intimacy that makes it possible. Objects, for example,
that are no more than cultural signs in some shows
become invested with new meanings in the new shows.
In the Bunker home a refrigerator, a chair, a dining
table, and the bathroom have become symbolic objects, a direct development from their use as plot device in more typical domestic comedy. They have
become objects that define a particular social class or
group rather than the reflection of an idealized, gen-
eralized expression of cultural taste. They are now
things that belong to and define this particular group
of individuals. Similarly, our knowledge of the characters goes beyond a formulaic response. Jim Ander-

son, of "Father Knows Best," was a type, his responses defined by cultural expectation. Archie Bunker is an individual. Each time we see him lose a bit of his façade we realize that his apparently one-dimensional character is the result of his choice, his own desire to express himself to the world in this persona. With his guard down we realize that he cares about his wife, in spite of the fact that he treats her miserably most of the time.

In the mini-series of the BBC the technical aspects of this sort of intimacy have been used to explore the idea itself and have resulted in moments of great symbolic power. In the adaptation of Henry James's *The Golden Bowl*, for example, we begin with a novel crucially concerned with problems of intimacy. The series is then filled with scenes that develop the idea visually. Such a sequence occurs during the days before Adam Verver asks Charlotte to be his wife. Though he does not realize it, Charlotte had at one time been the mistress of his daughter's husband, the Prince. She is considerably younger than Verver, and in order to establish a claim for her marriage, he suggests that they spend time together, in the most decorous manner, in his country home and in Brighton. In the midst of rooms filled with candles, furniture, paintings, and ornaments, the camera isolates them. Even in the huge ornate rooms they are bound together, the unit of our focus. One evening as Charlotte turns out the lamps, pools of light illuminate them, circled in the large dark rooms.

In one of the most crucial scenes of this sequence the camera moves along the outside of an elegant restaurant. Through the rain, through the windows, couples are framed at dining tables. A waiter arrives at Verver's table as the camera stops its tracking motion.

The couple begins to laugh; we hear them faintly as if through the actual window. Then, apparently at Verver's request, the waiter reaches across the table and closes the drapes. We are shut out of the scene, and we realize how closely we have been involved in the "action." We are made more aware of private moments. In the closing scene of the episode the camera movement is repeated. This time, however, Charlotte has agreed to the marriage and the couple is celebrating. Again we are outside. But as the episode ends, we remain with Verver and Charlotte, participating in their lamplit laughter.

Finally, this same motif is used in another episode. Charlotte and the Prince have again become lovers. They meet for a last time, realizing that their secret is known. The camera frames their hands, meeting in a passionate grip. It is like an embrace and it fills the entire screen. Suddenly the camera pulls back and the two people are shown in an actual embrace. Again, suddenly, the camera zooms out and the couple is seen from outside the window. It is raining again, as it was in Brighton, and a rapid torrent of water floods over the window, blurring the picture in a powerful sexual image.

Clearly, in the adaptation of a novel so concerned with matters of intimacy, the attempt has been to convey that concern with a set of visual images. In "The Waltons," however, we are reminded that this visual technique parallels a set of values that we have found operating in popular television throughout our survey of formulas. Intimacy, within the context of family, is a virtue, and when "The Waltons" uses specific techniques to make us aware of intimacy, it is to call our attention not to the form, but to the ideas, of the show.

In that series each episode closes with a similar

sequence. John Boy sits in his room writing in his journal. He has learned the requirement of solitude for his work, and his room has become a sacred space into which no one else intrudes. Other children in the family must share rooms, but he lives and works alone in this one. At the close of each story he narrates for us the meaning that he has drawn from the experience. We see him through a window as his voice comes over the visual track in the form of an interior monologue. As he continues to talk, the camera pulls back for a long shot of the house. It sits at the edge of the forest like a sheltered gathering place. It conveys the sense of warmth and protection, and even when there has been strain among the members of the family, we know that they have countered it as they counter their social and financial problems and that they will succeed. John Boy's window is lighted, usually the only one in the otherwise darkened home. As his speech ends, his light also goes out. We are left with the assurance of safety and love, as if we have been drawn by this calm ending into the family itself.

This sense of direct involvement can be enhanced by another factor in the television aesthetic, the idea of continuity. The sort of intimacy described here creates the possibility for a much stronger sense of audience involvement, a sense of becoming a part of the lives and actions of the characters they see. The usual episodic pattern of television only gives the illusion of continuity by offering series consisting of twenty-six individual units. The series may continue over a period of years, revolving around the actions of a set of regular characters. As pointed out, however, there is no sense of continuous involvement with these characters. They have no memory. They cannot change in response to events that occur within a weekly installment, and consequently they have no history. Each episode is self-contained with its own beginning and ending. With the exception of soap operas, television has not realized that the regular and repeated appearance of a continuing group of characters is one of its strongest techniques for the development of rich and textured dramatic presentations.

This lack of continuity leads to the central weakness of television, the lack of artistic probability. We have seen that many shows now deal with important subject matter. Because the shows conclude dramatically at the end of a single episode, and because the necessity for a popular response calls for an affirmative ending, we lose sight of the true complexity of many of the issues examined. This need not be the case, however, for we have seen two ways in which television can create a necessary sense of probability which can enhance the exploration of ideas and themes.

Probability in television may come in two major ways. The first is the one with which we are most familiar. We see the same characters over and over each week. Often it is this factor that is most frustrating in its refusal to develop probability among the characters. But in a series such as "All in the Family" this becomes an advantage, for the Bunkers continually encounter new experiences. Though most of the episodes are thematically related to the idea of Archie's bigotry, we have seen in analysis some of the ways in which reactions are changed. Some of the shifts may be starkly bitter, a strong departure for television comedy. Similarly, the continual introduction of new characters who appear on a regular basis allows the world to grow around the central family.

Even the slight shifts in more formulaic shows, such as "Owen Marshall" or "Marcus Welby," aid in this direction when the characters appear on one another's shows. The appearance is of a world of multiple dimensions.

Another sort of probability is made possible by the creation of continued series. The soap operas provide the key to this understanding, and even though they are distorted by their own stereotypical views, the values of the shows are expressed far more clearly because of the continuous nature of the programming. Even with the distortions the shows offer a value system that may be closer to that of the viewer than he or she is likely to find in prime-time programming.

The BBC productions, however, adaptations of novels and original historical re-creations, offer a much more rounded sense of probability. As with historical fiction and movies, these productions are interpretations. Anyone who has watched the TV versions of the great novels is aware that choices and selections have been made in the adaptation of one medium to another. In both cases the result has been the creation of a new work of art. The central innovative factor in these productions has been their refusal to be dominated by the hour-long time slot. They do not end in a single episode. They range from the twenty-six episodes of "The Forsyte Saga" to three- or five-week adaptations of other novels. In this way we are allowed a far more extensive examination of motivation, character, and event than we are in the traditional television time period. The extension of time allows for a fuller development of the idea of intimacy, for we are allowed a broader as well as a deeper look at individuals. The use of narrators to deal with compressed time has been highly effective, especially in "The Search for the Nile."

These factors indicate that the real relationship with other media lies not in movies or radio, but in the novel. Television, like the literary form, can offer a far greater sense of density. Details take on importance slowly, and within repeated patterns of action, rather than with the immediacy of other visual forms. It is this sense of density, built over a continuing period of time, that offers us a fuller sense of a world fully created by the artist.

Continuity, then, like intimacy, is a conceptual as well as a technical device. It, too, grows out of popular television and finds its fullest expression in the newer shows. The third factor that helps to define the aesthetic quality of television is also essential to its less sophisticated formulas, for we have seen from the very beginning how television has been dependent on the uses of history for much of its artistic definition.

The importance of history to the popular arts has been carefully dealt with by John Cawelti in an essay, "Mythical and Historical Consciousness in Popular Culture" (unpublished essay, 1971). The root of this distinction, which Cawelti takes from myth theorists such as Mircea Eliade, lies in the perception of time. In the mythical consciousness "time is multidimensional. Since mythical events exist in a sacred time which is different from ordinary time, they can be past and present and to come all at the same time" (ibid., p. 11). For modern man, however, history is unilinear and moves "from the past, through the present, and into the future" (ibid.).

Within the popular arts one can discover a similar distinction, and as an example might compare two types of Westerns. Resembling the mythical conscious-

ness is the Lone Ranger. "Though from time to time
the audience is reminded that the Lone Ranger
brought law and order to the West, the advance of
civilization plays a negligible role in the hero's adventure. . . . Instead . . . the manner of presenting the
saga of the masked hero reflects the multi-dimensional
time of the mythical consciousness" (ibid., p. 12).
The contrasting example is Owen Wister's *The Vir-
ginian* in which ". . . the symbols and agents of ad-
vancing civilization play a primary role in the story.
Indeed, they are commonly a major cause of the conflicts which involve the hero" (ibid.).

Another type of modification occurs among works
that might be grouped within the mythical dimen-
sion. It is this form that depends most strongly on a
sense of shared cultural values. At times as the values
themselves begin to change there must be a shift in
expression.

. . . to achieve the mythical sense in its traditional
form, the writer must create and maintain a highly
repetitive almost ritualistic pattern. This is one reason
why series characters like Deadwood Dick, The Lone
Ranger, and Hopalong Cassidy in regularly issued
publications or weekly programs have been such a
successful format for popular formulas. But the
potency of such ritual-like repetitions depends on
the persistence of underlying meanings. In ancient
societies the fixed patterns of myth reflected continuity of values over many generations. In modern
America, however, one generation's way of embodying the mythical pattern in cultural conventions tends
to become the next generation's absurdities.
[Ibid., p. 5]

It is the sort of shift in expression defined here that
is most important for the television formulas we have

examined. Shifts in underlying meanings occur more frequently than in the past, and instead of the changing patterns of generational attitudes it is almost as if America discovers new sets of values overnight. There seems to be little sense of value consensus. In spite of this, television manages to entertain vast numbers of viewers with patterns of action and with characters who seem familiar to the cultural consciousness.

Our analyses have shown, however, that there is little resemblance, in terms of underlying meaning, between the Western or the mystery as we know them on TV and the forms from which they emerge in literature, cinema, and radio. Similarly, the creation of special versions of families, of certain types of doctors and lawyers, indicates a type of formula that can cut across value distinctions and definitions that might have been embodied in these various formulas at one time.

The television formula requires that we use our contemporary historical concerns as subject matter. In part we deal with them in historical fashion, citing current facts and figures. But we also return these issues to an older time, or we create a character from an older time, so that they can be dealt with firmly, quickly, and within a system of sound and observable values. That vaguely defined "older time" becomes the mythical realm of television.

The 1973 season premier of "Gunsmoke" offered us all the trappings of the mythic and historical Western. There was a great deal of "on location" film (a common practice for season openers of the show, which then returns to the studio for most of the season) so that the environment created its sense of agency. The central plot involved the stealing of white women by Comancheros, and all the traditional villains, heroes, good and bad Indians appeared. The dual focus of the show, however, forced us to consider a thoroughly contemporary version of the problem. In one conflict we were concerned with the relationship of an orphaned child and a saloon girl. In the end the problems are resolved as the saloon girl gives up her own way of life in order to stay on a lonely ranch with the child and her grandfather. In another conflict we were concerned with the relationships of another orphan, a young man raised as a criminal by the Comanchero leader. In the end this young man must kill his surrogate father, escape with a haughty white girl, and be killed by her as he waits to ambush Marshal Dillon. In his dying words he says that he must have been a "damned fool" to believe that the girl loved him enough to overcome her class snobbery and go away with him. The ambiguity here forced us to admit the degree of goodness in the two outlaws and the saloon girl, to condemn racism in many versions, and to come to terms with the problems of the orphans in a particular social setting.

Although such generational and class conflicts could arise in any time and in any culture, they are framed so as to call attention to our own social problems. What has happened is that we have taken a contemporary concern and placed it, for very specific reasons, in an earlier time, a traditional formula. There the values and issues are more clearly defined. Certain modes of behavior, including violent behavior, are more permissible.

Detectives serve the same function. Ironside's fatherlike qualities aid in the solution of problems traditionally associated with the detective role. They also allow him to solve personal problems which appear to be large-scale versions of our own. Either by working out difficulties within his own "family team" or by working with the criminal or by working at the root cause of the crime, he serves as an appropriate authority figure for a society in which authority is both scarce and suspect.

In an even more striking television adaptation of history, we see families in domestic comedy behave as if they lived in an idealized nineteenth-century version of America. And our doctors and lawyers are easily associated with that same period. As if our time somehow mythically coexisted with that of an easier age, we create forms that speak in opposition to their contemporary settings. We turn our personal and social problems over to the characters who can solve them, magically, in the space of an enclosed hour. We have, in effect, created a new mythic pattern. It cuts across all the formulas with which we are familiar, transforming them and changing their force. Our own history is the one we see in these types, not the history common to the formula itself. Our history is all too familiar and perplexing, so to deal with it we have created the myth of television.

This aspect of television formula has enhanced the popularity of many widely viewed and accepted shows. Doubtless, one reason for the popularity of these successful series is the way in which they deal with contemporary problems in a self-conscious manner. They are highly "relevant" programs. They purport to question many issues. Such questioning is obviated, however, by the very structure of the shows. Always, the problems are solved. In most cases they are solved by the heroic qualities of the central characters. Whether the heroics take on the sterner aspects of frontier marshals or the gentler visage of kindly doctors, the questions that we take to our television stars are answered for us satisfactorily.

As with the other factors we can turn again to the newer shows to see the fuller development of the aesthetic sense of the use of history. With "The Waltons" it is possible to see a number of linked factors with the sense of history at the core. We are admitted to a tightly knit circle; we are intimately involved with a family, the central symbol of television. Because we share experiences with them, watch the children grow and deal specifically with the problems of growth and development, there is a strong sense of continuity to the series. The continuity is enhanced by a sense of community, of place and character, developed by different aspects of the series.

The great power of the program, however, develops out of its historical setting, the America of the Great Depression of the 1930s. The show demonstrates that the Depression period now carries with it a sense of mythical time. Frozen in the memory of those who experienced it, and passed on to their children, it is crucial to a sense of American cultural history, popular as well as elite. Indeed, it is crucial in part because it is the period that determines many contemporary American values. Much of the power of the show rises out of the realization that that time was much like our own—fragmented and frightening.

Like other mythical times, this period becomes, for television, a frame in which to examine our own problems. But the Depression does not yet have the qualities of the Western or detective story. Because it was a time of failure more than of success, it does not purport to offer heroic solutions to the problems. The solutions are those of "common" people, and we know that we will see the same characters in the following week and that they will have other problems of a variety not found in Westerns, mysteries, doctor and lawyer shows. Consequently there is little of the sense of a world made right by the power of the wise father. In the larger sense the continuing social context of the show, the unresolved Depression, brings to bear the feeling of a larger ill that cannot be corrected by strong, authoritative figures such as detectives and marshals.

The productions in the Masterpiece Theater series go a step further and refuse to offer firm final solutions to many problems confronted in the content of the shows. Many of the works raise complex moral and social issues. In many of them the central characters, far from serving as paternalistic guides and problem-solvers, die in the end. History is used here both to insulate the audience from the immediate impact of these unresolved issues and to demonstrate, at the same time, that the issues are universal, unbounded by history and defined by the fact that we are all human.

Finally, in shows such as "All in the Family" the mythical frame dissolves and the history we see is our own. Again, the sense of that history is strong and is a crucial part of the show. Our sense of class and economic reality, the distinctions among groups of persons within American society, allows us to confront problems directly. To a degree the comic context replaces the comforting removal of a more remote time. But by breaking the frame of the typical situation or domestic comedy, by questioning the very premises on which television is built, these shows force the audience into some sort of evaluation of its own beliefs. Their consistently high ratings indicate that the television audience is ready to become involved in entertainment that allows at least some of its members a more immediate examination of values and attitudes than is allowed by more traditional forms.

The interrelationships among these shows, the historical and comparative relationships between simpler and more sophisticated versions of formulas, indicate that television is in the process of developing a range of artistic capabilities that belies the former one-dimensional definitions. The novel can offer entertainment from Horatio Alger to Herman Melville, mysteries from Spillane to Dostoevski. The cinema can range from Roy Rogers Westerns to *Cries and Whispers*. So, too, can television offer its multiple audiences art from the least questioning, most culturally insulated situation comedy to "All in the Family," from "Adventures in Paradise" to "The Search for the Nile," from "The Guiding Light" to "The Forsyte Saga."

In the past one did not speak of any television programs as "art." The aesthetic viewpoint was ignored, at times excluded from the process of understanding and explaining the extraordinarily powerful economic, social, and psychological effects of television. But it should no longer be possible to discuss "violence on television" without recognizing the aesthetic structure within which that violence occurs. It should no longer be possible to categorize the audience in terms of social and cultural values without examining the artistic context of those values as presented on television.

Intimacy, continuity, and a special sense of history are not the sole defining aesthetic attributes in the broad world of televised entertainment. Like many of the popular arts, television is the expression of multiple talents. Good writing, fine acting, technical excellence, and the sure hand of directors and producers go into making the best of television. Similarly, production necessities, overtaxed writers, formulaic actors, and imitative directors and producers can contribute to the worst of it. But intimacy, continuity, and history are devices that help to distinguish how television can best bring its audience into an engagement with the content of the medium. It is precisely because the devices are value expressions themselves, and because the content of television is replete with values, judgments, and ideas deeply imbedded in our culture that we must continually offer new and supplementary ways of observing, describing, and defining it. In this manner we can better understand how television is different from other media. We can begin to understand how it has changed the style and content of popular entertainment into forms of its own, and we can examine the ways in which those forms have changed within television's own development. For more than three decades we have viewed television from many perspectives without having come to grips with what it is for most of its audience. TV is America's most popular art. Its artistic function can only grow and mature, and as it does, so must its popularity.

BIBLIOGRAPHY OF WORKS CITED

Bogart, Leo. *The Age of Television*. New York: Frederick Ungar, 1956.

Casty, Alan. *Mass Media and Mass Man*. New York: Holt, Rinehart and Winston, 1968.

Cawelti, John. *The Six-Gun Mystique*. Bowling Green, Ohio: Bowling Green University Popular Press, 1970.

——. "Mythical and Historical Consciousness in Popular Culture." Unpublished Essay, 1971.

Columbia Broadcasting System. Press Release. New York, August 1973.

Cooke, Alistair. Comments to the audience of Episode Twelve of "America: A Personal History." Maryland Institute College of Art, April 1973, Baltimore, Maryland.

Deer, Irving and Harriet. *The Popular Arts, A Critical Reader*. New York: Scribner's, 1967.

De Forest, Lee. *Television: Today and Tomorrow*. New York: Dial Press, 1942.

Elliott, William Y., ed. *Television's Impact on American Culture*. East Lansing, Michigan: Michigan State University Press, 1956.

Glynn, Eugene David. "A Psychiatrist Looks at Television." *Television's Impact on American Culture*, East Lansing, Michigan, 1956.

Hamner, Earl. "Acceptance Speech." National Association of Television Program Executives, March 1974, quoted in *Facts, Figures & Film*, April 1974.

Hentoff, Margot. "The Forsyte Saga: artful if not art." *Vogue*, January 1, 1970.

Hutchinson, Thomas H. *Here Is Television: Your Window to the World*. New York: Dial Press, 1946.

Kaplan, Abraham. "The Aesthetics of the Popular Arts." *The Popular Arts, A Critical Reader*, New York, 1967.

Katz, Elihu, and David Foulkes. "The Use of Mass Media as 'Escape': Clarification of a Concept." *Public Opinion Quarterly,* Fall 1962 pp. 377–88.

Lion, John R. "Always the Violence." Baltimore *Sun,* February 18, 1973.

McCray, Curtis. "Kaptain Kronkite: The Myth of the Eternal Frame." Paper presented at the Popular Culture Association Convention, East Lansing, Michigan, April 1971.

McDonald, Dwight. "A Theory of Mass Culture." *Mass Media and Mass Man,* New York, 1968.

McLuhan, Marshall. *The Gutenberg Galaxy.* Toronto: University of Toronto Press, 1962.

——. *Understanding Media.* New York: McGraw-Hill, 1964.

Menaker, Dan. "Art and Artifice in Network News." *Harper's,* October 1972.

Nixon, Agnes Eckhardt. "In Daytime TV the Golden Age Is Now." *Television Quarterly,* Winter 1972.

Schramm, Wilbur, et al. *Television in the Lives of Our Children.* Stanford: Stanford University Press, 1961.

Shayon, Robert Lewis. *Open to Criticism.* Boston: Beacon Press, 1971.

Skornia, Harry J. *Television and Society.* New York: McGraw-Hill, 1965.

Steiner, Gary. *The People Look at Television.* New York: Knopf, 1963.

Van Den Haag, Ernest. "Of Happiness and Despair We Have No Measure." *Mass Media and Mass Man,* New York, 1968.

INDEX